PRACTICAL GOURMET
Small Plates For Sharing

Pictured on front cover:
Tostada Cups With Lemony Lentils And Spinach, page 20

Nutrition Information Guidelines
Each recipe has been analyzed using the Canadian Nutrient File from Health Canada,
which is based upon the United States Department of Agriculture (USDA) Nutrient
Database.
- If more than one ingredient is listed (such as "hard margarine or butter"), or if a range
  is given (1 - 2 tsp., 5 - 10 mL), only the first ingredient or first amount is analyzed.
- The lesser number of servings is used if a range is stated.
- Ingredients indicating "sprinkle," "optional" or "for garnish" are not included in the
  nutrition information.
- Milk used is 1% M.F. (milk fat), unless otherwise noted.

Vera Mazurak, Ph.D (Nutritionist)

Practical Gourmet
Small Plates For Sharing
Copyright © Company's Coming Publishing Limited

First Printing October 2008

Library and Archives Canada Cataloguing in Publication
Small plates for sharing.
(Practical gourmet)
Includes index.
Edited by Laurie Stempfle.
ISBN 978-1-897069-74-5
1. Appetizers. 2. Tapas. 3. Cookery, International.
I. Stempfle, Laurie II. Series.
TX740.S593 2008   641.8'12   C2008-900371-3

Published by
Company's Coming Publishing Limited
2311 – 96 Street
Edmonton, Alberta, Canada T6N 1G3
Tel: 780-450-6223   Fax: 780-450-1857
www.companyscoming.com

Company's Coming is a registered trademark owned by
Company's Coming Publishing Limited

Printed in China

We acknowledge the financial support of the Government of Canada through the Book Publishing Industry
Development Program (BPIDP) for our publishing activities.

Acknowledgements

Small Plates For Sharing was created through the dedicated efforts of the people listed below:

Editor-in-Chief	Laurie Stempfle
Research and Development Manager	Jill Corbett
Editorial Director	Tabea Berg
Editor, Recipe Editor	Janet Fowler
Senior Food Editor	Lynda Elsenheimer
Food Editors	Mary Anne Korn
	Eleana Yun
Researcher	Frieda Lovig
Senior Recipe Tester	James Bullock
Recipe Testers	Allison Dosman
	Audrey Smetaniuk
Proofreader	Laurie Penner
Contributors	Diane Barton
	Rita Feutl
	Roxanne Higuchi
	Amy Hough
	Hank Leonhardt
	Patricia Meili-Bullock
	Aaron Taylor
Creative Director	Heather Markham
Design Lead	Michelle Loewen
Design and Production	Kim Deley
Director of Photography	Jason Symington
Photography	Stephe Tate Photo
Food Stylist	Ashley Billey
Prop Stylist	Snez Ferenac
Prep Assistant	Linda Dobos
Production Supervisor	Matt Bromley
Nutritionist	Vera Mazurak, Ph.D
Founding Author	Jean Paré
President	Grant Lovig
Vice President, Production and Creative	Alanna Wilson

We gratefully acknowledge the following suppliers for their generous support of our test and photo kitchens:

Broil King Barbecues	*Hamilton Beach® Canada*	*Proctor Silex® Canada*
Corelle®	*Lagostina®*	*Tupperware®*

Our special thanks to the following businesses for providing numerous props for photography:

Stokes	*Mikasa Home Store*	*Danesco Inc.*
Winners Stores	*Emile Henry*	*Wal-Mart Canada Inc.*
The Bay	*Canhome Global*	*Klass Works*
Pier 1 Imports®	*Totally Bamboo*	*Out of the Fire Studio*
Cherison Enterprises Inc.		

Contents

Beds & Pillows   10

Piquant nibbles cradled by vegetables, bread or pastry

• Roasted Spinach Portobellos • Spiced Jam With Heady Garlic And Cambozola • Creamy Wild Mushrooms On Pastry Points • Wild Rice Blini • Tostada Cups With Lemony Lentils And Spinach • Potato Crostini With Caramelized Bacon • Five-Spiced Crepes With Coconut Scallops • Pear Puff Tart • Shrimp With Horseradish Beet Coulis • Grecian Beef Pastries • Open-Faced Tilapia Po' Boy

Little Bowls   34

Heady dips, hot and cold soups, rich risottos and succulent mélanges

• Creole Crab Fondue • Panini Sticks With Dipping Trio • Shrimp Bisque • Sun-Dried Tomato And Leek Mussels • Smoked Salmon Blintz Cups • Mango Gazpacho • Cambozola Custard With Mushroom Port Compote • Coconut Chili Soup • Miso Mushroom Risotto With Scallops • Butter Chicken With Spinach And Pappadums

Maverick Morsels   56

Inspired twists on favourite flavours

• Seared Beef Carpaccio With Peppercorn Mushrooms • Peanut Noodle Cakes With Sweet Chili Prawns • "Uptown" Goat Cheese Potato Skins • Sweet Polenta Fries With Chipotle Lime Dip • Walnut Pesto-Crusted Lamb With Cranberry Port Jus • Margarita Chicken Lollipops • Chili Chili Cocoroons • Crab Sushi Squares • Spiced Panko Chicken With Tropical Rum Dip • Savoury Shortbread Trio • Fiery Plantain Chips With Cocomango Dip • Walnut Ginger Crisps • Halibut Bites In Peppered Panko Crust • Shrimp Corn Cakes With Lime Sauce

On The Green   86

Glorious ways with leafy and vegetable greens

• Almond Brie Croutons On Apple-Dressed Spinach • Smoked Tuna And Wasabi Cream In Endive Boats • Seared Scallops Verde • Warm Ginger Chicken Over Spinach • Praline Pecans, Beets And Blue Cheese On Baby Greens • Miso-Glazed Cod On Ginger-Spiked Cucumbers • Ruby Chard With Jerk Cornmeal Tofu "Croutons" • Salmon With Herb Sabayon • Citrus-Glazed Lobster And Fennel • Chili Squid On Peas And Peppers • Herb Olive Feta Mélange Over Grilled Asparagus • Caramel Pork Tenderloin On Bok Choy

The Company's Coming Legacy

Jean Paré grew up with an understanding that family, friends and home cooking are the key ingredients for a good life. A busy mother of four, Jean developed a knack for creating quick and easy recipes using everyday ingredients. For 18 years, she operated a successful catering business from her home kitchen in the small prairie town of Vermilion, Alberta, Canada. During that time, she earned a reputation for great food, courteous service and reasonable prices. Steadily increasing demand for her recipes led to the founding of Company's Coming Publishing Limited in 1981.

The first Company's Coming cookbook, *150 Delicious Squares*, was an immediate bestseller. As more titles were introduced, the company quickly earned the distinction of publishing Canada's most popular cookbooks. Company's Coming continues to gain new supporters in Canada, the United States and throughout the world by adhering to Jean's Golden Rule of Cooking: *Never share a recipe you wouldn't use yourself.* It's an approach that has worked— millions of times over!

A familiar and trusted name in the kitchen, Company's Coming has extended its reach throughout the home with other types of books and products for everyday living.

Though humble about her achievements, Jean Paré is one of North America's most loved and recognized authors. The recipient of many awards, Jean was appointed Member of the Order of Canada, her country's highest lifetime achievement honour.

Today, Jean Paré's influence as founding author, mentor and moral compass is evident in all aspects of the company she founded. Every recipe created and every product produced upholds the family values and work ethic she instilled. Readers the world over will continue to be encouraged and inspired by her legacy for generations to come.

Foreword

Good company and great food create a powerful combination. When laughter and conversation mix with the heady fragrance and flavours of delicious fare, we are not just sharing a meal—we are nourishing our lives. Artfully prepared dishes awaken the senses and please the palate. And here's the secret: It can all be so simple!

Company's Coming is delighted to introduce Practical Gourmet, a new series designed to help home cooks create no-fuss, sumptuous food. It is possible to wow both the eye and the palate using readily available ingredients and minimal effort. Practical Gourmet offers sophisticated recipes without the hassle of complicated methods, special equipment or obscure ingredients. Cook because you want to, the way you want to.

Each title features full-page colour photos of every recipe, menu suggestions, sidebars on preparation tips and tricks, how-to photos, imaginative presentation ideas and helpful entertaining information to allow you and your guests to really savour the food—and your time together.

Small Plates For Sharing is an appropriate "starter" for the series. The focus is on smaller portions—think tapas, hors d'oeuvres or antipasto. Novice cooks and experienced chefs will value the range of flavours, ethnic influences, gorgeous photographs and step-by-step instructions.

The French have a name for a small bite with big impact—amuse bouche—literally, something that amuses the mouth. In the following eight chapters, great care and attention have been given to combinations of flavour, texture and presentation so that you and your guests can explore great food possibilities, one delicious mouthful after another.

Guests will appreciate your thoughtfulness and skill, while you revel in how easy it was to prepare these impressive morsels. *Small Plates For Sharing* lets you cook and entertain in a relaxed atmosphere—and have fun doing it.

Approachable recipes, fabulous results, wonderful get-togethers—it all starts with *Small Plates For Sharing*.

Atmosphere. A fantastic cocktail gets your guests in the mood for socializing and sets the tone for the evening. Whether it be a simple, classic martini or an elaborate and colourful cocktail, this will be the first taste your guests enjoy. Here are a few favourites to try, each with a modern twist on tradition.

Libations

Blue Lagoon

Pour 1 part white (light) rum, 1/2 part lychee liqueur and 2 parts orange juice over ice in a chilled cocktail glass. Add 1 tsp. (5 mL) lemon juice and top with club soda. Drizzle with 1 part blue-coloured, bitter orange liqueur and allow it to settle to the bottom.

Bueno Beer Margaritas

In a pitcher, combine a 12 oz. (341 mL) can of limeade concentrate with equal parts water, beer and tequila. Add 1/4 cup (60 mL) orange liqueur. Serve over crushed ice in margarita glasses.

Canadian Snowbird

Pour 1 part Canadian whiskey (rye), 4 parts apple juice and 1/2 part each of peach schnapps, lemon liqueur and maple syrup over ice in a chilled cocktail glass. Squeeze a lemon wedge over top and drop in.

Orange Truffletini

Combine 1 part vanilla vodka, 1 part chocolate liqueur and 1/2 part orange liqueur in a martini glass.

Mojitos

Using a wooden spoon, crush or "muddle" 3 cut-up limes with 40 mint leaves and 1/4 cup (60 mL) granulated sugar in a 1 quart (1 L) pitcher. Add 1/4 cup (60 mL) lime cordial, if desired, to make a sweeter cocktail. Stir in 6 oz. (170 mL) rum and add ice until pitcher is 3/4 full. Top with club soda. Serve in cocktail glasses.

Piña Colada Martini

Combine 1 part coconut rum, 3/4 part orange vodka and 2 parts pineapple juice with crushed ice in a cocktail shaker. Shake and strain into a cocktail glass. Drop in a cherry and add a drizzle of grenadine.

Pomcosmo

Combine 2 parts lemon vodka, 2 parts pomegranate juice and 1 part orange liqueur with crushed ice in a cocktail shaker. Shake and strain into a cocktail glass.

Inviting. The allure of these morsels may put you in mind of sweet dreams, but their fulsome flavours will enliven your senses. Discover savoury delights nestled on canapé beds of bread, pastry—even mushroom caps, beet coulis or potato crostini. Like Goldilocks before you, you can experiment: Which bed and which pillow are just right for you?

Beds & Pillows

Piquant nibbles cradled by vegetables, bread or pastry

Roasted Spinach Portobellos

Large portobello mushrooms, gills removed (see Tip, below)	2	2
Butter-flavoured cooking spray		
Bacon slices, diced	2	2
Chopped fresh spinach leaves, lightly packed	2 cups	500 mL
Basil pesto	3 tbsp.	50 mL
Fine dry bread crumbs	2 tbsp.	30 mL
Grated Italian cheese blend	3/4 cup	175 mL
Pine nuts	2 tsp.	10 mL
Prepared marinara pasta sauce	1/4 cup	60 mL

Remove and chop mushroom stems. Set aside. Spray both sides of mushroom caps with cooking spray and place, stem-side down, on a baking sheet. Bake in a 375°F (190°C) oven for 10 minutes.

Cook bacon in a frying pan until crisp. Add mushroom stems and cook for about 5 minutes until softened and liquid is evaporated.

Stir in spinach leaves and pesto and cook until spinach is softened. Remove from heat.

Stir in bread crumbs and half of cheese. Spoon into mushroom caps. Sprinkle with remaining cheese and pine nuts. Bake for 10 to 15 minutes until heated through and golden. Cut into quarters.

Swirl some marinara sauce on a serving plate. Arrange mushroom wedges over sauce, drizzling remaining sauce over top. Makes 8 wedges.

1 wedge: 123 Calories; 9.0 g Total Fat (1.4 g Mono, 0.6 g Poly, 3.1 g Sat); 13 mg Cholesterol; 5 g Carbohydrate; 1 g Fibre; 6 g Protein; 216 mg Sodium

GARNISH
sprig of fresh basil

TIP
Because the gills can sometimes be bitter, be sure to remove them from the portobellos before stuffing. First remove the stems, then, using a small spoon, scrape out and discard the mushroom gills.

EXPERIMENT!
Use a prepared bruschetta mix in place of marinara sauce for a different taste and texture.

Stuffed mushrooms are always a crowd-pleaser. Using large portobellos in place of smaller mushrooms makes for a unique presentation and easier prep. Pairs perfectly with other Italian-flavoured small plates.

Spiced Jam

With Heady Garlic And Cambozola

Olive oil	1 tsp.	5 mL
Chopped onion	1/2 cup	125 mL
Garlic clove, minced	1	1
Ginger marmalade	3 tbsp.	50 mL
Tomato paste	2 tbsp.	30 mL
Chili paste (sambal oelek)	3/4 tsp.	4 mL
Ground cinnamon	1/4 tsp.	1 mL
Ground cumin	1/4 tsp.	1 mL
Garlic bulbs, roasted (see How To, below)	2	2
Long baguette bread slices, toasted	8	8
Cambozola cheese	4 oz.	113 g

Heat olive oil in a frying pan on medium. Add onion and garlic and cook for about 5 minutes until onion is softened.

Add next 5 ingredients and stir until heated through. Transfer to a serving bowl.

Arrange remaining 3 ingredients on a serving platter with jam. Serves 4.

1 serving: 292 Calories; 16.0 g Total Fat (2.7 g Mono, 0.5 g Poly, 7.6 g Sat); 30 mg Cholesterol; 30 g Carbohydrate; 2 g Fibre; 7 g Protein; 318 mg Sodium

---

ABOUT CAMBOZOLA
Cambozola is a blue cheese that was developed in Germany in the 1970s. A cross between Camembert and Gorgonzola, Cambozola is a soft cheese with a notably smooth, creamy texture and light blue veins. It has a mild flavour, unlike the strong pungent sharpness of Stilton or Gorgonzola.

HOW TO ROAST GARLIC
To roast garlic, trim 1/4 inch (6 mm) from each bulb to expose tops of cloves, leaving bulbs intact. Wrap bulbs individually in greased foil and bake in 375°F (190°C) for about 45 minutes until tender. Let stand until cool enough to handle.

A tantalizing tango of **tastes** and **textures** is created
when **zippy** jam is partnered with rob... garlic
and **bold** Cambozola. The **smell** of roastin... ...c
whets the appetite in **anti**...**tion**
of something sp...

Creamy Wild Mushrooms
On Pastry Points

Package of puff pastry (14 oz., 397 g), thawed according to package directions	1/2	1/2
Butter	2 tbsp.	30 mL
Chopped fresh shiitake mushrooms	3 cups	750 mL
Chopped fresh oyster mushrooms	2 cups	500 mL
Finely chopped onion	1/3 cup	75 mL
Garlic clove, minced	1	1
Salt	1/4 tsp.	1 mL
Pepper	1/8 tsp.	0.5 mL
Dry sherry	3 tbsp.	50 mL
Chopped fresh thyme	1/2 tsp.	2 mL
Whipping cream	2/3 cup	150 mL

Roll out pastry to a 12 x 5 inch (30 x 12.5 cm) rectangle. Cut crosswise into 6 rectangles. Cut rectangles diagonally to form triangles and arrange on a baking sheet. Bake in a 400°F (205°C) oven for 15 to 20 minutes until golden. Let stand until cool.

Melt butter in a frying pan on medium-high. Add next 6 ingredients and cook for about 15 minutes until onion is soft and mushrooms are browned.

Stir in sherry, thyme and cream. Serve over pastry points. Serves 6.

1 serving: 288 Calories; 22.2 g Total Fat (3.7 g Mono, 0.5 g Poly, 10.6 g Sat); 44 mg Cholesterol; 17 g Carbohydrate; 2 g Fibre; 5 g Protein; 307 mg Sodium

---

GARNISH
sprigs of fresh thyme

EXPERIMENT!
Changing the variety of mushroom changes the flavour of your dish. Using wild mushrooms makes for an earthier flavour, while using white mushrooms makes for a milder flavour. In dishes like this one, opt for maximum impact and select more flavourful mushrooms. Experiment and create your own variations by trying different combinations of fresh wild mushrooms. You should find several varieties in your grocery store or produce market.

A rich flavour and an **elegant** presentation.
Sometimes the **simplest things** yield
the most **fantastic results.**

Wild Rice Blini

Large egg, fork-beaten	1	1
Milk	2 tbsp.	30 mL
Chopped cooked wild rice	1/4 cup	60 mL
Chopped capers	1 tbsp.	15 mL
Pepper	1/4 tsp.	1 mL
Buttermilk pancake mix	1/3 cup	75 mL
Cooking oil	2 tsp.	10 mL
Spreadable cream cheese	3 tbsp.	50 mL
Finely chopped fresh dill	1 tsp.	5 mL

Combine first 5 ingredients in a bowl. Stir in pancake mix until just mixed.

Heat cooking oil in a small frying pan on medium. Spoon half of batter into the pan, tilting and swirling pan to ensure bottom is covered. Cook for 1 to 2 minutes until edges appear dry and bubbles form on top. Turn pancake. Cook for 1 to 2 minutes until golden. Transfer to cutting board. Repeat with remaining batter. Using a 2 inch (5 cm) cookie cutter, cut out 7 circles from each pancake.

Combine cream cheese and dill. Spoon about 3/4 tsp. (4 mL) onto each circle. Makes 14 blini.

1 blini: 38 Calories; 2.2 g Total Fat (0.9 g Mono, 0.3 g Poly, 0.9 g Sat); 17 mg Cholesterol; 3 g Carbohydrate; trace Fibre; 1 g Protein; 92 mg Sodium

---

GARNISH
smoked salmon slivers
sprigs of fresh dill

ABOUT BLINI
These small pancakes originally come from Russia and were traditionally yeast-risen and made with buckwheat flour. They are often served with sour cream and caviar or smoked salmon. Blini have much history, dating back to the Middle Ages. Involved in many significant ceremonial events including the Butter Festival, which took place the week before Lent, blini was eaten twice a day as a treat.

Soft little pancakes filled with chewy wild rice
and tangy capers are easily made using pancake mix.
Cutting small rounds from two larger pancakes is a smart shortcut
for perfectly sized blini.

Tostada Cups
With Lemony Lentils And Spinach

Flour tortilla (9 inch, 22 cm, diameter)	1	1
Cooking spray		
Cooking oil	1/2 tsp.	2 mL
Finely chopped onion	1/4 cup	60 mL
Granulated sugar	1/4 tsp.	1 mL
Canned lentils, rinsed and drained	1/2 cup	125 mL
Chopped fresh spinach leaves, lightly packed	1/2 cup	125 mL
Finely chopped roasted red pepper	2 tsp.	10 mL
Herb and garlic cream cheese	1 tbsp.	15 mL
Grated lemon zest	1 tsp.	5 mL
Salt	1/4 tsp.	1 mL
Pepper, sprinkle		

Spray both sides of tortilla with cooking spray and cut into 8 wedges. Press wedges into 8 muffin cups with points sticking out (see How To, below). Bake in a 450°F (230°C) oven for about 5 minutes until golden and crisp.

Heat cooking oil in a frying pan on medium. Add onion and sugar and cook until lightly browned.

Stir in next 3 ingredients and cook until spinach starts to wilt.

Stir in remaining 4 ingredients. Spoon into tostada cups. Makes 8 tostada cups.

1 tostada cup: 43 Calories; 1.5 g Total Fat (0.2 g Mono, 0.1 g Poly, 0.6 g Sat); 2 mg Cholesterol; 6 g Carbohydrate; 1 g Fibre; 2 g Protein; 118 mg Sodium

HOW TO MAKE TOSTADA CUPS

GARNISH
roasted red pepper strips
lemon peel

What makes this dish so **conversational** is the **interesting** use of tortilla shells to create toasty little cups. Be as **inventive** as you like and **create** your own fillings.

Potato Crostini
With Caramelized Bacon

Baby potatoes, ends trimmed and cut in half crosswise	8	8
Olive oil	1 tbsp.	15 mL
Salt	1/4 tsp.	1 mL
Brown sugar, packed	1/2 cup	125 mL
Dried crushed chilies	1 tsp.	5 mL
Bacon slices	10	10
Sour cream	1/4 cup	60 mL
Cream cheese, softened	2 tbsp.	30 mL
Dijon mustard	1/2 tsp.	2 mL
Dried crushed chilies	1/4 tsp.	1 mL

Toss first 3 ingredients together in a bowl, then spread evenly on a baking sheet. Bake in a 400°F (205°C) oven for about 25 minutes until potatoes are tender. Arrange potatoes, trimmed-side down, on a serving plate. Reduce oven temperature to 350°F (175°C).

Combine brown sugar and first amount of chilies. Coat bacon slices with the brown sugar mixture. Arrange on a wire rack set in a foil-lined baking sheet. Bake for about 25 minutes until browned and glazed. Let stand for 10 minutes before finely chopping bacon.

Combine remaining 4 ingredients and bacon. Spoon onto potatoes. Makes 16 potato crostini.

1 potato crostini: 135 Calories; 3.9 g Total Fat (1.7 g Mono, 0.4 g Poly, 1.5 g Sat); 8 mg Cholesterol; 22 g Carbohydrate; 2 g Fibre; 4 g Protein; 145 mg Sodium

---

GARNISH
sprigs of parsley

Roasted baby potatoes make for an **interesting twist** on traditional bread crostini. **Caramelizing** the bacon adds sweetness to the **smokiness**. Try using a combination of red and white potatoes for an appealing **colour** contrast.

Five-Spiced Crepes
With Coconut Scallops

Large egg	1	1
Milk	1/2 cup	125 mL
All-purpose flour	6 tbsp.	100 mL
Butter, melted	1 1/2 tbsp.	25 mL
Granulated sugar	1/2 tsp.	2 mL
Chinese five-spice powder	1/4 tsp.	1 mL
Cooking oil	1 1/2 tsp.	7 mL
Sesame oil	2 tsp.	10 mL
Coarsely chopped scallops	1 cup	250 mL
Chopped green onion	2 tbsp.	30 mL
Seasoned salt	1/2 tsp.	2 mL
Coconut milk	1/2 cup	125 mL
Cornstarch	1 tsp.	5 mL

Using a blender or food processor, process first 6 ingredients until smooth. Let stand for 30 minutes.

Heat 1/4 tsp. (1 mL) cooking oil in a small frying pan on medium. Pour about 2 tbsp. (30 mL) batter into pan. Immediately tilt and swirl pan to ensure bottom is covered. Cook for about 1 minute until brown spots appear. Transfer to a plate. Repeat with remaining batter, heating cooking oil between batches to prevent sticking. Fold crepes into quarters and arrange on a serving plate.

Heat sesame oil in the same frying pan on medium. Add next 3 ingredients and cook for 1 minute. Combine coconut milk and cornstarch and add to the pan. Heat and stir for about 1 minute until scallops are opaque and sauce is bubbling. Spoon over crepes. Serves 6.

1 serving: 171 Calories; 11.1 g Total Fat (2.6 g Mono, 1.3 g Poly, 6.3 g Sat); 52 mg Cholesterol; 9 g Carbohydrate; trace Fibre; 9 g Protein; 222 mg Sodium

---

GARNISH
toasted sesame seeds
green onion

ABOUT CHINESE FIVE-SPICE POWDER
This popular spice blend is used extensively in Chinese cooking. A pungent mixture of five different spices, usually cinnamon, cloves, fennel seed, star anise and Szechuan peppercorns, its flavour is quite distinct. You should easily find five-spice powder in your grocery store or Asian market.

An **exotic** and **intriguing** flavour experience. The scent of **aromatic spices** will give your guests just a **hint** of what they are about to **enjoy**.

Pear Puff Tart

Package of puff pastry (14 oz., 397 g), thawed according to package directions	1/2	1/2
Granulated sugar	1 tbsp.	15 mL
Crumbled Stilton cheese	1/2 cup	125 mL
Medium fresh unpeeled pear, thinly sliced	1	1
Butter, melted	1 tsp.	5 mL
Coarsely ground pepper, sprinkle		

Roll out pastry to a 7 x 11 inch (18 cm x 28 cm) rectangle and transfer to a baking sheet. Sprinkle with sugar.

Sprinkle with cheese, leaving a 1/2 inch (12 mm) border. Arrange pear slices over cheese. Brush with butter and sprinkle with pepper. Bake in a 400°F (205°C) oven for 20 to 25 minutes until golden. Cut into 8 pieces.

1 piece: 184 Calories; 12.1 g Total Fat (5.5 g Mono, 1.2 g Poly, 3.9 g Sat); 8 mg Cholesterol; 16 g Carbohydrate; 1 g Fibre; 3 g Protein; 160 mg Sodium

ABOUT STILTON

Stilton is one of Britain's most well-known cheeses. Made from whole cow's milk, its sharp, nutty flavour strengthens during the four to six months it ages before being sold. Stilton is creamy and crumbly with a pale yellow interior, blue-green veins and a crusty brownish rind. White Stilton is also available, it is not aged as long, so no veins develop.

A perfect **combination** of sweet and savoury
flavours on a bed of golden, buttery **pastry**.
For a different **presentation**, serve the tart whole and
allow your guests to cut their own **portions**.

Shrimp

With Horseradish Beet Coulis

Uncooked extra-large shrimp (peeled and deveined)	12	12
Montreal steak spice	1 tsp.	5 mL
Olive oil	2 tsp.	10 mL
Can of whole baby beets, puréed with 3 tbsp. (50 mL) juice	14 oz.	398 mL
Butter, melted	2 tbsp.	30 mL
Prepared horseradish	1 tbsp.	15 mL
Chopped fresh dill	2 tsp.	10 mL
Arugula leaves, lightly packed	1/4 cup	60 mL

Combine shrimp and steak spice. Let stand for 15 minutes. Heat olive oil in a frying pan on medium. Add shrimp and cook until pink.

Combine next 4 ingredients and pour onto a serving plate.

Arrange arugula and shrimp over top. Serves 4.

1 serving: 122 Calories; 8.4 g Total Fat (3.2 g Mono, 0.6 g Poly, 4.0 g Sat); 47 mg Cholesterol; 7 g Carbohydrate; 1 g Fibre; 5 g Protein; 484 mg Sodium

---

HOW TO DEVEIN SHRIMP
To devein shrimp, strip off the legs and peel away the shell. Using a small, sharp knife, make a shallow cut along the centre of the back. Rinse under cold water to wash out the dark vein.

A **feast** for the eyes and the **palate** with strong, **bold** flavours and **vibrant** colours— perfect for a **sophisticated** get-together.

Grecian Beef Pastries

Olive oil	1 tsp.	5 mL
Lean ground beef	1/2 lb.	225 g
Chopped red onion	1/2 cup	125 mL
Chopped red pepper	1/2 cup	125 mL
Sun-dried tomato pesto	2 tbsp.	30 mL
Lemon juice	2 tsp.	10 mL
Garlic clove, minced	1	1
Salt	1/4 tsp.	1 mL
Pepper	1/2 tsp.	2 mL
Grated lemon zest	1 tsp.	5 mL
Package of puff pastry (14 oz., 397 g), thawed according to package directions	1/2	1/2
Chopped pitted kalamata olives	1/4 cup	60 mL
Crumbled feta cheese	1/2 cup	125 mL
Chopped fresh oregano	1 tbsp.	15 mL

Heat olive oil in a frying pan on medium. Add next 8 ingredients and scramble-fry until beef is no longer pink. Remove from heat.

Stir in lemon zest and let stand until cool.

Roll out pastry to a 12 x 12 inch (30 x 30 cm) square. Cut into 12 rectangles and transfer to a greased baking sheet. Sprinkle with beef mixture, leaving a 1/4 inch (6 mm) border. Press down gently.

Sprinkle with olives and cheese. Bake in a 400°F (205°C) oven for about 20 minutes until pastry and cheese are golden.

Sprinkle with oregano. Makes 12 pastries.

1 pastry: 165 Calories; 11.0 g Total Fat (5.6 g Mono, 1.0 g Poly, 3.7 g Sat); 17 mg Cholesterol; 10 g Carbohydrate; 1 g Fibre; 6 g Protein; 304 mg Sodium

---

GARNISH
lemon wedges

TIP
Be sure to add fresh herbs at the end of cooking or as a garnish for maximum flavour impact.

EXPERIMENT!
Vary the flavour and make it with lamb instead of beef. You could also try seasoned or marinated feta instead of plain.

Opa! Make it a completely Greek experience by serving a **rich** red wine or a shot of **ouzo** with these **sensational** little pastries.

Open-Faced Tilapia Po' Boy

Large egg	1	1
Water	1 tbsp.	15 mL
Fine dry bread crumbs	1/4 cup	60 mL
Blackened (or Cajun) seasoning	1 tbsp.	15 mL
Tilapia fillets, any small bones removed (about 3 oz., 85 g, each), see Tip, below	4	4
Cooking oil	2 tbsp.	30 mL
Mayonnaise	1/2 cup	125 mL
Tangy dill relish	2 tbsp.	30 mL
Spicy mustard (with whole seeds)	2 tbsp.	30 mL
Lemon juice	1 tbsp.	15 mL
Small dinner rolls, halved and toasted	6	6
Arugula leaves, lightly packed	1 cup	250 mL
Capers	1 tbsp.	15 mL

Beat egg and water in a shallow bowl. Combine bread crumbs and seasoning on a plate. Dip fillets into egg mixture and press into crumb mixture until coated.

Heat cooking oil in a large frying pan on medium-high. Cook fillets for about 2 minutes per side until browned and fish flakes easily when tested with a fork. Cut fillets into 3 pieces each.

Combine next 4 ingredients. Spread half of mayonnaise mixture on roll halves.

Arrange arugula and tilapia portions on roll halves. Drizzle with remaining mayonnaise mixture. Sprinkle with capers. Makes 12 po' boys.

1 po' boy: 192 Calories; 9.4 g Total Fat (5.1 g Mono, 2.7 g Poly, 1.1 g Sat); 32 mg Cholesterol; 20 g Carbohydrate; 1 g Fibre; 8 g Protein; 545 mg Sodium

---

TIP
Look for the thin fillets of tilapia that are often available in the frozen section of your grocery store. If you are unable to find small fillets, you can purchase larger fillets that add up to the same weight and cut them into appropriate-sized portions after cooking.

A **scaled-down** version of the **po' boy** sandwich for a taste of **Mardi Gras**. Serve with hot sauce on the side and cold beer or **lemonade**.

Complex. There is much ado about small *plates*, but not all scrumptious fare sits on the surface. Rich treasures lie below and are worth digging for. Pick up a fork or spoon and see what you can unearth. Delicious plunder is ready to be discovered in these pots of gourmet gold. Dishes with such depth truly need to be explored and experienced.

Little Bowls

Heady dips, hot and cold soups, rich risottos and succulent mélanges

Creole Crab Fondue

Cream cheese, softened	1/3 cup	75 mL
Mayonnaise	1/3 cup	75 mL
Finely chopped celery	3 tbsp.	50 mL
Finely chopped green onion	2 tbsp.	30 mL
Dijon mustard (with whole seeds)	1 tbsp.	15 mL
Creamed horseradish	1 tsp.	5 mL
Old Bay seasoning	1 tsp.	5 mL
Cayenne pepper	1/4 tsp.	1 mL
Crabmeat, cartilage removed	1/2 lb.	225 g
Grated mozzarella cheese	1/3 cup	75 mL
Fine dry bread crumbs	1/4 cup	60 mL

Combine first 8 ingredients. Stir in crabmeat and transfer to a 2 cup (500 mL) baking dish.

Combine cheese and bread crumbs and sprinkle over top. Bake in a 400°F (205°C) oven for about 20 minutes until bubbling and golden. Serves 6.

1 serving: 180 Calories; 13.2 g Total Fat (5.4 g Mono, 2.4 g Poly, 4.2 g Sat); 24 mg Cholesterol; 6 g Carbohydrate; trace Fibre; 9 g Protein; 523 mg Sodium

ABOUT CREOLE AND CAJUN FOOD
They're both spicy, but what's the difference? Although the ingredients can be similar, the origins are different. Creole cooking is based on French traditions, but with influences from Spain, Africa, Germany, Italy and the West Indies. Creole fare was developed by people of various nations and cultures who settled in and around New Orleans. Cajun cooking was developed by the Acadians as they learned to live in south Louisiana after being sent away from Nova Scotia. The Acadians (later known as Cajuns) tended to serve food prepared from locally available ingredients and often cooked in one pot. Cajun cuisine is a cooking style which reflects these people's ingenuity, creativity, adaptability and survival instinct.

Put a little **fire** in your fondue.
If you have some **brave** guests, hand them a bottle
of **hot sauce** to add even more intensity to
this already **spicy** dip. Serve with veggie sticks.

Panini Sticks
With Dipping Trio

Extra-virgin olive oil	1 tbsp.	15 mL
Finely chopped fresh rosemary	1 tsp.	5 mL
Dried marjoram, crushed	1 tsp.	5 mL
Square panini breads (8 x 8 inches, 20 x 20 cm, each)	2	2
Coarse salt, sprinkle		
SUN-DRIED TOMATO DIP		
Tzatziki sauce	1/3 cup	75 mL
Sun-dried tomato pesto	2 tsp.	10 mL
Chili paste (sambal oelek)	1/4 tsp.	1 mL
LEMON AIOLI DIP		
Roasted garlic mayonnaise	1/3 cup	75 mL
Lemon juice	2 tsp.	10 mL
Grated lemon zest	1 tsp.	5 mL
TZIKI HERB DIP		
Tzatziki sauce	1/3 cup	75 mL
Chopped fresh dill	1 1/2 tsp.	7 mL
Chopped fresh mint	1 1/2 tsp.	7 mL
Lemon pepper	1/2 tsp.	2 mL

Combine first 3 ingredients and brush on panini breads. Cut into 1 inch (2.5 cm) wide strips and arrange, close together, on a baking sheet. Sprinkle with salt. Bake in a 400°F (205°C) oven for about 8 minutes until edges are crisp.

Sun-Dried Tomato Dip: Combine all 3 ingredients.

Lemon Aloli Dip: Combine all 3 ingredients.

Tziki Herb Dip: Combine all 4 ingredients.

Serve dips with panini sticks. Serves 8.

1 serving: 222 Calories; 15.4 g Total Fat (3.2 g Mono, 4.1 g Poly, 1.8 g Sat); 13 mg Cholesterol; 31 g Carbohydrate; 1 g Fibre; 3 g Protein; 366 mg Sodium

---

GARNISH
sprig of basil
lemon peel
sprig of mint

PRESENTATION INSPIRATION
Provide individual plates so guests can serve themselves a spoonful of each dip. This way guests can sample all three—and it will help to avoid the temptation to double-dip!

Sometimes picking up a **convenience** product and adding
a few simple **embellishments** is all it takes to truly make it your own.
This very shareable **treat** is just as easy to make as it is to **enjoy**.

Shrimp Bisque

Butter	1 tbsp.	15 mL
Uncooked medium shrimp (peeled and deveined), tails intact	6	6
Finely chopped celery	1/4 cup	60 mL
Finely chopped shallots	1/4 cup	60 mL
Uncooked shrimp (peeled and deveined), chopped	3 oz.	85 g
Can of tomato sauce	7 1/2 oz.	213 mL
Whipping cream	1/3 cup	75 mL
Dry white wine	1/4 cup	60 mL
Chopped fresh tarragon	1/2 tsp.	2 mL
Fresh tarragon leaves	6	6

Melt butter in a saucepan on medium. Add first amount of shrimp and cook until pink. Transfer to a plate and set aside.

Add celery and shallots to the same saucepan and cook for about 5 minutes until softened.

Stir in next 5 ingredients. Simmer, covered, on medium-low for 5 minutes. Using a hand blender, process until smooth (see Safety Tip, below). Pour into 6 small serving cups.

Place 1 shrimp and 1 tarragon leaf over each cup of soup. Serves 6.

1 serving: 104 Calories; 6.9 g Total Fat (1.9 g Mono, 0.4 g Poly, 4.2 g Sat); 53 mg Cholesterol; 4 g Carbohydrate; 1 g Fibre; 5 g Protein; 268 mg Sodium

---

SAFETY TIP
We recommend that you not use a countertop blender to process hot liquids.

ABOUT SHRIMP
Shrimp are sold according to size, but keep in mind that the perception of size varies from region to region, as well as between fish markets. As a general guideline, these are the number of shrimp you can expect to get from a 1 lb. (454 g) measure:

- Jumbo   11 – 15
- Extra-large   16 – 20
- Large   21 – 30
- Medium   31 – 35
- Small   36 – 45
- Baby   about 100

Elegant and rich-tasting bisque is most satisfying when sampled in small portions. These little bowls truly taste like traditional bisque, but take much less time to prepare.

Sun-Dried Tomato And Leek Mussels

Mussels	1 lb.	454 g
Olive oil	1 1/2 tsp.	7 mL
Finely chopped leek (white part only)	1/2 cup	125 mL
Garlic clove, minced	1	1
Dried crushed chilies	1/8 tsp.	0.5 mL
Dry white wine	3/4 cup	175 mL
Sun-dried tomato pesto	2 tbsp.	30 mL

Lightly tap to close any mussels that are opened 1/4 inch (6 mm) or more. Discard any that do not close.

Heat olive oil in a saucepan on medium. Add next 3 ingredients and cook for about 5 minutes until leek is softened.

Stir in wine and pesto. Bring to a boil and add mussels. Cook, covered, for about 5 minutes until mussels are opened. Discard any unopened mussels. Serves 4.

NOTE: For safety reasons, it is important to discard any mussels that do not close before cooking, as well as any that have not opened during cooking.

1 serving: 98 Calories; 2.4 g Total Fat (1.4 g Mono, 0.4 g Poly, 0.4 g Sat); 8 mg Cholesterol; 7 g Carbohydrate; 1 g Fibre; 4 g Protein; 406 mg Sodium

---

GARNISH
chopped fresh chives

ABOUT MUSSELS
When cooking with mussels, there are a few points to keep in mind:

- Use only mussels with tightly closed shells. If the shells are slightly open, tap them lightly. If they don't close, don't cook them.
- Discard any mussels with broken shells.
- Avoid mussels that feel heavy, as they are often filled with sand.
- Don't use mussels that feel too light or loose when shaken.
- Shucked mussels should be plump, with clear liquid.
- Smaller mussels tend to be more tender than larger ones.
- Discard any mussels that do not open during cooking.

Plump, juicy **mussels**
bathe in a pesto, wine and leek **sauce**.
Serve with **crusty** French bread
for **dipping**.

Smoked Salmon Blintz Cups

Ricotta cheese	1/2 cup	125 mL
Chopped smoked salmon	1/4 cup	60 mL
Cream cheese, softened	1/4 cup	60 mL
Chopped fresh dill	1 tbsp.	15 mL
Pepper	1/4 tsp.	1 mL
All-purpose flour	1 cup	250 mL
Baking powder	1 tsp.	5 mL
Salt	1/4 tsp	1 mL
Large eggs	3	3
Milk	1/3 cup	75 mL
Butter, melted	2 tbsp.	30 mL
Granulated sugar	2 tbsp.	30 mL

Combine first 5 ingredients. Set aside.

Combine next 3 ingredients in a small bowl. Make a well in the centre.

Whisk next 4 ingredients in a separate bowl and add to the well. Whisk until smooth. Pour about 1/4 cup (60 mL) batter into each of 6 greased 6 oz. (170 mL) ramekins. Carefully spoon salmon mixture over batter. Pour remaining batter over top. Bake in a 350°F (175°C) oven for 15 to 18 minutes until slightly puffed but firm to the touch. Let stand for 5 minutes before removing blintz cups from ramekins to a serving plate. Makes 6 blintz cups.

1 blintz cup: 227 Calories; 11.6 g Total Fat (3.6 g Mono, 0.7 g Poly, 6.4 g Sat); 122 mg Cholesterol; 21 g Carbohydrate; trace Fibre; 10 g Protein; 299 mg Sodium

---

GARNISH
sprigs of fresh dill
red pepper slivers

ABOUT GARNISHING
Why garnish? It's sad to say, but not all food looks as good as it tastes. Garnishing helps to add a little bit of extra colour or artistic flair to your food. Garnishes don't always have to be placed directly on your food either. Sometimes they can be placed underneath or around the food, decorating the plate itself. Keep in mind that a garnish should not only be attractive, it should also reflect the flavours of the dish you're serving it with. That way, your guests get a hint about what flavours to expect.

Blintzes are known for being labour-intensive, but we've found a **great** way to make them without all the fuss. **Creamy** smoked salmon **filling** hides inside a rich, golden **batter** for an **unforgettable** flavour.

Mango Gazpacho

Chopped mango (see Tip, below)	1 cup	250 mL
Orange juice	1/3 cup	75 mL
Chopped fresh cilantro	1 tbsp.	15 mL
Lime juice	1 tbsp.	15 mL
Brown sugar, packed	1/2 tsp.	2 mL
Finely grated gingerroot	1/2 tsp.	2 mL
Ground cumin	1/2 tsp.	2 mL
Salt	1/2 tsp.	2 mL
Pepper	1/8 tsp.	0.5 mL
Diced English cucumber (with peel)	1/4 cup	60 mL
Diced mango	1/4 cup	60 mL
Diced red pepper	1/4 cup	60 mL

In a blender or food processor, process first 9 ingredients until smooth.

Stir in remaining 3 ingredients. Chill, covered, for about 1 hour until cold. Pour into 4 small serving cups. Serves 4.

1 serving: 51 Calories; 0.3 g Total Fat (0.1 g Mono, 0.1 g Poly, 0.1 g Sat); 0 mg Cholesterol; 13 g Carbohydrate; 1 g Fibre; 1 g Protein; 295 mg Sodium

TIP
For faster prep, use frozen mango. Chop it up while it's still icy and you'll save time on the chill factor.

ABOUT GAZPACHO
Originating from southern Spain, gazpacho's conventional form usually contains tomatoes. Served cold, this refreshing puréed soup can be either smooth or chunky. Today, there are many versions of this elegant dish—including sweeter ones.

A cool, upbeat take on gazpacho. **Mango** is the hero in this **chilled** soup with cilantro as the **sidekick**. There's something distinctively **modern** about the pairing of these two **flavours**.

Cambozola Custard
With Mushroom Port Compote

Cambozola cheese (rind removed), cut up	2 oz.	57 g
Half-and-half cream	1 cup	250 mL
Large eggs	2	2
Salt	1/4 tsp.	1 mL
Olive oil	2 tsp.	10 mL
Chopped white mushrooms	2 cups	500 mL
Finely chopped onion	1 cup	250 mL
Garlic cloves, minced	2	2
Salt	1/2 tsp.	2 mL
Pepper	1/4 tsp.	1 mL
Port	1/2 cup	125 mL

Combine cheese and cream in a saucepan. Heat on medium until cheese is melted. Let stand for 10 minutes.

Slowly whisk in eggs and salt until smooth. Pour into 4 greased 3 to 4 oz. (85 to 114 mL) ramekins and place in an 8 x 8 inch (20 x 20 cm) baking dish. Carefully pour boiling water into the baking dish until water comes halfway up sides of ramekins (see How To, below). Bake in a 325°F (160°C) oven for about 20 minutes until centres only wobble slightly. Transfer ramekins to a wire rack and let stand until slightly cooled. Invert onto 4 serving plates.

Heat olive oil in a frying pan on medium. Add next 5 ingredients and cook until mushrooms are browned. Stir in port. Simmer for about 1 minute until thickened. Spoon alongside custards. Serves 4.

1 serving: 277 Calories; 18.1 g Total Fat (4.8 g Mono, 0.9 g Poly, 9.1 g Sat); 131 mg Cholesterol; 13 g Carbohydrate; 1 g Fibre; 8 g Protein; 585 mg Sodium

HOW TO ASSEMBLE CUSTARDS

GARNISH
fresh chives

Silky and smooth, this dish is also **heady**, bold and **robust**—a wonderful blend of **flavours** that provides a wake-up call for the **senses**.

Coconut Chili Soup

Sesame oil	2 tsp.	10 mL
Finely chopped onion	1/2 cup	125 mL
Garlic clove, minced	1	1
Thai red curry paste	1/2 tsp.	2 mL
Coconut milk	1 cup	250 mL
Prepared vegetable broth	1/2 cup	125 mL
Brown sugar, packed	1 tsp.	5 mL
Soy sauce	1 tsp.	5 mL
Lime juice	3/4 tsp.	4 mL

Heat sesame oil in a saucepan on medium. Add next 3 ingredients and cook for about 5 minutes until onion is softened.

Stir in next 4 ingredients. Simmer, covered, for 10 minutes to blend flavours. Remove from heat.

Stir in lime juice. Using a hand blender, process until smooth (see Safety Tip, page 40). Strain into 4 small serving bowls and discard solids. Serves 4.

1 serving: 158 Calories; 15.2 g Total Fat (1.4 g Mono, 1.1 g Poly, 11.7 g Sat); 0 mg Cholesterol; 6 g Carbohydrate; trace Fibre; 1.7 g Protein; 155 mg Sodium

GARNISH
Thai hot chili peppers
hot chili oil

Transport yourself to the **tropics** with this smooth, **velvety** soup. The intensity comes from Thai red **curry** paste—just enough to really **heat** things up.

Miso Mushroom Risotto
With Scallops

Sesame oil	2 tsp.	10 mL
Chopped fresh shiitake mushrooms	2 cups	500 mL
Chopped green onion	1/4 cup	60 mL
Dry white wine	1/3 cup	75 mL
White miso	1 tbsp.	15 mL
Arborio rice	1/2 cup	125 mL
Water	1 1/3 cups	325 mL
Salt	1/2 tsp.	2 mL
Sesame oil	2 tsp.	10 mL
Large sea scallops	4	4
Sea salt	1/2 tsp.	2 mL

Heat first amount of sesame oil in a saucepan on medium. Add mushrooms and green onion and cook for about 8 minutes until mushrooms are browned.

Stir in wine and miso and cook until wine is almost all evaporated. Add rice and stir for 30 seconds.

Stir in water and salt. Bring to a boil. Simmer, covered, on medium-low for about 20 minutes, without stirring, until rice is tender. Let stand, covered, for 5 minutes.

Heat second amount of sesame oil in a frying pan on medium. Add scallops, sprinkle with sea salt and cook for about 3 minutes until scallops are opaque and browned. Stir risotto and divide into 4 small bowls, placing 1 scallop over top. Serves 4.

1 serving: 189 Calories; 5.4 g Total Fat (1.9 g Mono, 2.2 g Poly, 0.9 g Sat); 5 mg Cholesterol; 26 g Carbohydrate; 1 g Fibre; 7 g Protein; 738 mg Sodium

---

GARNISH
fresh chives

MAKE AHEAD
The risotto reheats well in the microwave, so it can be made in advance.

PRESENTATION INSPIRATION
Try serving the risotto in Asian-themed or small, square bowls. Have chopsticks available for your guests, but provide forks as well for any guests who lack confidence in their chopstick skills.

Get the conversation started with this **fascinating** sampling of **fusion cuisine**. Asian flavours of sesame and miso meet Italian risotto for an **intriguing union** of cultural cookery.

Butter Chicken
With Spinach And Pappadums

Tandoori curry paste	3 tbsp.	50 mL
Boneless, skinless chicken thighs, chopped	1/2 lb.	225 g
Butter	1 tbsp.	15 mL
Chopped onion	1 cup	250 mL
Diced Roma (plum) tomato	3/4 cup	175 mL
Butter	1 tbsp.	15 mL
Whipping cream	1/2 cup	125 mL
Chopped fresh spinach leaves, lightly packed	1 cup	250 mL
Chopped fresh cilantro	1 tbsp.	15 mL
Sliced almonds, toasted (see How To, page 208)	1 tbsp.	15 mL
Black peppercorn pappadums	8	8
Cooking spray		

Combine curry paste and chicken. Melt butter in a frying pan on medium. Add onion and chicken mixture and cook for about 10 minutes until onion is soft.

Add tomato and second amount of butter and cook until tomato is soft. Stir in cream. Simmer for about 10 minutes until thickened and reduced by half.

Stir in spinach and cook until wilted. Transfer to a serving bowl and sprinkle with cilantro and almonds.

Spray both sides of pappadums with cooking spray. Broil, 2 at a time, for about 30 seconds until puffed. Turn pappadums. Broil for about 10 seconds until golden. Serve with chicken. Serves 4.

1 serving: 322 Calories; 26.9 g Total Fat (6.9 g Mono, 1.9 g Poly, 12.2 g Sat); 90 mg Cholesterol; 14 g Carbohydrate; 2 g Fibre; 13 g Protein; 493 mg Sodium

---

EXPERIMENT!
Pappadums come in a variety of flavours. Try experimenting with different types for this recipe. Some flavours you might find in your grocery store or Indian market include:

• Plain	• Cumin	• Cilantro	• White chili
• Garlic	• Sesame	• Green chili	• Red chili

Crisp pappadums make the **perfect base** for serving **miniature portions** of this popular Indian entrée. Consider serving this dish with samosas or Curried Cheese And Fruit Wheel (page 194) and Walnut Ginger Crisps (page 80).

Rebellious. Some things are just too original to be classified. These small plates defy tidy categories—and that puts them in a class of their own. Familiar dishes done new ways—like "Uptown" Goat Cheese Potato Skins or Crab Sushi Squares— are beguiling. Vibrant, daring, unique and sometimes entirely unexpected, these wickedly delicious bites are bound to thrill. You can't help it; the attraction is undeniable. Everyone secretly roots for the rebel.

Maverick Morsels

Inspired twists on favourite flavours

Seared Beef Carpaccio
With Peppercorn Mushrooms

Montreal steak spice	1 tbsp.	15 mL
Chopped fresh thyme	1 tbsp.	15 mL
Beef strip loin steak	1 lb.	454 g
Cooking oil	1 tbsp.	15 mL
Sliced brown mushrooms	5 cups	1.25 L
Brandy	1/3 cup	75 mL
Canned green peppercorns	1 tbsp.	15 mL
Butter	1 tbsp.	15 ml
Arugula leaves, lightly packed	1/2 cup	125 mL

Combine steak spice and thyme. Press steak into spice mixture until coated. Cook on a greased grill on high for about 2 minutes per side until browned and slightly crisp. Transfer to cutting board. Cover with foil and let stand for 10 minutes.

Heat cooking oil in a frying pan on medium-high. Add mushrooms and cook until browned and liquid is evaporated.

Stir in brandy and peppercorns. Add butter and stir until melted.

Cut steak across the grain into very thin slices. Arrange with arugula and mushrooms on a serving plate. Serves 6.

1 serving: 250 Calories; 15.7 g Total Fat (6.7 g Mono, 1.2 g Poly, 6.0 g Sat); 47 mg Cholesterol; 3 g Carbohydrate; 1 g Fibre; 17 g Protein; 391 mg Sodium

---

ALTERNATIVE METHOD
Instead of grilling the steak, you can sear it, using olive oil, in a very hot stainless steel or cast iron frying pan. Sear each side for only one minute. The result will be a very thin, dark crust that is quite appealing. However, it is not recommended that you use this method with a non-stick pan, as the high heat may ruin the non-stick coating.

Satiate your senses. Peppery, thinly sliced beef and mushrooms sautéed in **brandy** and **green peppercorns** unite with the natural zing of arugula.

Peanut Noodle Cakes
With Sweet Chili Prawns

Uncooked large shrimp (peeled and deveined), butterflied (see How To, below), tails intact	12	12
Sweet chili sauce	1/3 cup	75 mL
Water	3 tbsp.	50 mL
Soy sauce	1 tbsp.	15 mL
Large egg	1	1
Chunky peanut butter	1 tbsp.	15 mL
Thai red curry paste	1 1/2 tsp.	7 mL
Cooked spaghettini	2 cups	500 mL
Chopped fresh cilantro	2 tbsp.	30 mL
Chopped green onion	2 tbsp.	30 mL
Cooking oil	3 tbsp.	50 mL

Toss first 4 ingredients together in a bowl. Let stand for 10 minutes.

Whisk next 3 ingredients together in a medium bowl. Add next 3 ingredients. Toss together until well coated.

Heat cooking oil in a large frying pan on medium. Make 6 rounds of noodle mixture in the pan. Cook for about 5 minutes per side, pressing lightly to flatten, until crispy and golden. Transfer to a plate. Add shrimp mixture to the same frying pan and cook on medium-high for about 2 minutes until shrimp turn pink. Place 2 shrimp over each noodle cake and drizzle with pan juices. Serves 6.

1 serving: 200 Calories; 9.9 g Total Fat (5.1 g Mono, 2.8 g Poly, 1.2 g Sat); 52 mg Cholesterol; 20 g Carbohydrate; 1 g Fibre; 7 g Protein; 646 mg Sodium

HOW TO BUTTERFLY SHRIMP

GARNISH
chopped fresh cilantro
salted peanuts
lime wedges

Sure to spark **applause** and lively conversation, these **curiosity-piquing** noodle cakes will **delight** the cook as much in **cooking** as they delight the **guests** in **indulging**.

"Uptown" Goat Cheese Potato Skins

Medium unpeeled baking potatoes, baked and cooled	3	3
Olive oil	2 tbsp.	30 mL
Lemon pepper	1/2 tsp.	2 mL
Crumbled goat (chèvre) cheese	3/4 cup	175 mL
Grated havarti cheese	1/2 cup	125 mL
Butter	1 tbsp.	15 mL
Coarsely chopped capers	3 tbsp.	50 mL
Garlic cloves, thinly sliced	2	2
Sun-dried tomatoes in oil, blotted dry and finely chopped	1/3 cup	75 mL
Chopped fresh chives	2 tbsp.	30 mL
Chopped fresh oregano	1 tbsp.	15 mL

Cut potatoes into quarters lengthwise. Scoop away pulp, leaving a thin layer on each skin. Brush both sides of skins with olive oil and sprinkle with lemon pepper. Place, skin-side up, on a baking sheet. Bake in a 425°F (220°C) oven for about 7 minutes until starting to crisp. Turn over.

Sprinkle goat and havarti cheese over top. Bake for about 7 minutes until cheese is melted and golden. Arrange on a serving platter.

Melt butter in a frying pan on medium. Add capers and garlic and cook for about 5 minutes until garlic is golden. Spoon over potatoes.

Sprinkle with remaining 3 ingredients. Makes 12 potato skins.

1 potato skin: 127 Calories; 8.7 g Total Fat (2.4 g Mono, 0.3 g Poly, 4.7 g Sat); 15 mg Cholesterol; 7 g Carbohydrate; 1 g Fibre; 5 g Protein; 219 mg Sodium

TIME SAVER
Feel free to bake the potatoes a day in advance. Cooking the potatoes in the microwave is another option for added convenience. Just prick the potatoes in several places with a fork and wrap individually with paper towel. Microwave on high (100%) for 8 to 10 minutes until tender, turning the potatoes halfway through cooking.

Potato skins, not often invited to the better parties, become *de rigueur* as showier fare when melded with the rich and complementary flavours of lemon, capers and chèvre.

Sweet Polenta Fries
With Chipotle Lime Dip

Sour cream	1/4 cup	60 mL
Mayonnaise	1/4 cup	60 mL
Lime juice	2 tbsp.	30 mL
Chopped fresh cilantro	2 tbsp.	30 mL
Finely chopped chipotle pepper in adobo sauce (see Tip, page 202)	1 1/2 tsp.	7 mL
Grated lime zest	1/2 tsp.	2 mL
Coarse (sanding) sugar	1/4 cup	60 mL
Coarse sea salt	2 tbsp.	30 mL
Ground cumin	1 tbsp.	15 mL
Ground coriander	1 1/2 tsp.	7 mL
Cayenne pepper	1/2 tsp.	2 mL
Polenta roll	1.1 lb.	500 g
All-purpose flour	1/4 cup	60 mL
Cooking oil	3 cups	750 mL

Combine first 6 ingredients. Set aside.

Combine next 5 ingredients. Set aside.

Cut polenta roll into fries, about 1/2 inch (12 mm) thick. Gently toss in flour until coated.

Heat cooking oil in a large frying pan on medium-high (see How To, page 124). Shallow-fry polenta in batches, for about 5 minutes per batch, until golden. Transfer with a slotted spoon to paper towels to drain. While fries are still hot, toss with 1 tbsp. (15 mL) sugar mixture until coated. Serve with dip and remaining sugar mixture. Serves 6.

1 serving: 260 Calories; 15.9 g Total Fat (8.5 g Mono, 4.4 g Poly, 2.1 g Sat); 7 mg Cholesterol; 27 g Carbohydrate; 1 g Fibre; 3 g Protein; 2691 mg Sodium

TIP
Tossing items in flour before frying helps prevent them from sticking to each other.

ABOUT SANDING SUGAR
Sanding, or coarse, sugar tastes the same as granulated sugar—its difference lies purely in aesthetics. Because the sugar grain is larger, it sparkles or glints, giving an eye-catching appearance to whatever it's used on. It comes in a variety of colours—although the bright hues are more suited to desserts or confections.

Let your guests **enjoy** the interactive **experience** of dredging these **unique** cornmeal fries in a **sweet** and **spicy seasoning** before taking them for a dunk in the perfectly complementary dip.

Walnut Pesto-Crusted Lamb
With Cranberry Port Jus

Rack of lamb (8 ribs), bones Frenched (see Tip, below)	1	1
Salt, sprinkle		
Pepper, sprinkle		
Cooking oil	1 tsp.	5 mL
Ruby port	1 cup	250 mL
Cranberries	1/2 cup	125 mL
Balsamic vinegar	2 tsp.	10 mL
Whole-wheat bread slice	1	1
Chopped walnuts, toasted (see How To, page 208)	2 tbsp.	30 mL
Basil pesto	1 tsp.	5 mL
Butter, melted	1 tbsp.	15 mL
Dijon mustard	1 tbsp.	15 mL

Cover bones of lamb rack with foil (see Tip, below). Sprinkle with salt and pepper. Heat cooking oil in a frying pan on medium-high. Sear lamb until browned. Transfer to a plate.

Add port and cranberries to the same frying pan. Boil gently until reduced by half. Stir in vinegar. Transfer to a blender or food processor and process until smooth.

In a clean blender or food processor, process bread into coarse crumbs. Add walnuts and pesto and process until just combined. Transfer to a bowl. Drizzle with butter and toss until combined.

Brush meaty side of lamb with mustard. Press crumb mixture over the mustard. Bake, uncovered, in a 375°F (190°C) oven for 20 to 25 minutes until internal temperature reaches 135°F (57°C) or until meat reaches desired doneness. Cover with foil and let stand for 10 minutes. Cut lamb rack into 1-bone portions and serve with cranberry mixture. Serves 8.

1 serving: 150 Calories; 6.1 g Total Fat (2.0 g Mono, 1.4 g Poly, 2.2 g Sat); 30 mg Cholesterol; 7 g Carbohydrate; 1 g Fibre; 9 g Protein; 97 mg Sodium

TIP
When getting your lamb rack cut, ask the butcher to remove the chine bone (also known as the backbone). This will make the ribs much easier to slice and separate.

TIP
Cover any exposed bone with foil before roasting to help prevent darkening.

Delicate walnut-crusted chops in a
fruity *jus* will **tantalize** and **tease**—
just enough to **caress** the palate and still have it
yearning for the next taste **sensation**.

Margarita Chicken Lollipops

Tequila	1/2 cup	125 mL
Lime juice	1/4 cup	60 mL
Dried crushed chilies	1 tsp.	5 mL
Ground cumin	1 tsp.	5 mL
Chili powder	1/2 tsp.	2 mL
Garlic powder	1/2 tsp.	2 mL
Salt	1/2 tsp.	2 mL
Chicken drumettes, Frenched (optional), see How To, below	2 lb.	900 g
Cornstarch	2 tsp.	10 mL
Tequila	2 tbsp.	30 mL
Orange juice	1 tbsp.	15 mL
Liquid honey	1 tbsp.	15 mL
Grated lime zest	1 tsp.	5 mL

Combine first 7 ingredients in a large resealable freezer bag. Add drumettes and marinate for 4 hours. Drain marinade into a saucepan. Simmer on medium for 5 minutes.

Stir cornstarch into tequila and orange juice. Add to simmering marinade mixture and stir until bubbling and thickened. Stir in honey and lime zest. Arrange drumettes on a foil-lined baking sheet. Brush marinade mixture over drumettes. Bake in a 425°F (220°C) oven for about 20 minutes, brushing occasionally with marinade mixture, until no longer pink inside. Makes about 16 drumettes.

1 drumette: 162 Calories; 9.1 g Total Fat (trace Mono, trace Poly, 2.4 Sdt); 43 mg Cholesterol; 2 g Carbohydrate; trace Fibre; 10 g Protein; 117 mg Sodium

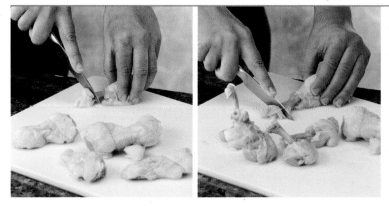

HOW TO FRENCH DRUMETTES
Use a sharp knife to loosen the meat and skin from the skinny end of the drumette. Gently push the skin and meat toward the fat end of the drumette, cleanly exposing the bone. Remove any bits of fat.

GARNISH
lime wedges

You'll be **pleased** to bring these **drumettes** to your fiesta with their **exceptional** flavouring and **unique** **presentation**—your guests will be too **curious** to miss out.

Chili Chili Cocoroons

Egg whites (large), room temperature	2	2
Granulated sugar	1/4 cup	60 mL
Medium unsweetened coconut	1/2 cup	125 mL
Chili paste (sambal oelek)	1 tsp.	5 mL
Grated lime zest	1/2 tsp.	2 mL
Mango chutney, finely chopped (or sweet chili sauce)	1 tbsp.	15 mL

Beat egg whites until soft peaks form. Gradually add sugar, beating constantly until stiff peaks form (see How To, below).

Fold in next 3 ingredients until combined. Spoon 12 equal portions onto a parchment paper-lined baking sheet. Press small indents into tops. Bake in a 325°F (160°C) oven for about 15 minutes until golden.

Spoon mango chutney into indents. Makes 12 cocoroons.

1 cocoroon: 42 Calories; 2.1 g Total Fat (0.1 g Mono, trace Poly, 1.8 g Sat); 0 mg Cholesterol; 5 g Carbohydrate; 1 g Fibre; 1 g Protein; 32 mg Sodium

**HOW TO SPOT
SOFT AND STIFF PEAKS**

These **deceptively savoury** cookies will first **surprise** and then **intrigue** your guests as they sample the **delicious** combination of **coconut** and mango **balanced** with **chili** heat.

Crab Sushi Squares

Japanese-style (sushi) rice	3/4 cup	175 mL
Water	1 cup	250 mL
Mirin	1 1/2 tbsp.	25 mL
Rice vinegar	1 1/2 tbsp.	25 mL
Granulated sugar	1 tbsp.	15 mL
Black sesame seeds	1/2 tsp.	2 mL
Salt	1/2 tsp.	2 mL
Nori (roasted seaweed) sheet	1	1
Large ripe avocado, thinly sliced	1	1
Can of frozen crabmeat, thawed and squeezed dry, cartilage removed	11 oz.	320 g
Mayonnaise	3 tbsp.	50 mL
Chili paste (sambal oelek)	1 tsp.	5 mL
Black sesame seeds, sprinkle		

Combine rice and water in a small saucepan. Bring to a boil. Simmer, covered, on medium-low for 20 minutes, without stirring. Remove from heat and let stand, covered, for 10 minutes. Transfer to a bowl.

Stir next 5 ingredients until sugar is dissolved. Add to rice and mix well. Line the bottom of an 8 x 8 inch (20 x 20 cm) baking dish with foil, allowing foil to overhang on opposite sides.

Place nori sheet in baking dish, cutting to fit if necessary. Firmly press rice mixture over nori.

Arrange avocado slices over top.

Combine next 3 ingredients and spread over avocado. Sprinkle with sesame seeds. Chill, covered, for 1 hour. Use overhanging foil to remove sushi from the baking dish (see How To, below) and cut into 16 squares.

1 square: 81 Calories; 3.5 g Total Fat (2.0 g Mono, 0.7 g Poly, 0.4 g Sat); 1 mg Cholesterol; 9 g Carbohydrate; trace Fibre; 4 g Protein; 236 mg Sodium

HOW TO REMOVE SUSHI

GARNISH
red pepper slivers
fresh cilantro leaves

Experience sushi **layered** rather than rolled, for a familiar California roll flavour with a **unique** and **stylish** presentation. Accompany with **pickled ginger** or wasabi for the sushi enthusiasts in your crowd.

Spiced Panko Chicken
With Tropical Rum Dip

Olive oil	1/4 cup	60 mL
Dijon mustard	3 tbsp.	50 mL
Montreal steak spice	1 tsp.	5 mL
Boneless, skinless chicken breasts, cut into ten 1 inch (2.5 cm) wide strips, about 3 inches (7.5 cm) long	3/4 lb.	340 g
Panko crumbs	1 1/2 cups	375 mL
Paprika	1/2 tsp.	2 mL
Cooking spray		
Pineapple orange juice	1 1/2 cups	375 mL
Brown sugar, packed	1/4 cup	60 mL
Coconut rum	2 tbsp.	30 mL
Dijon mustard	2 tsp.	10 mL

Combine first 3 ingredients in a large resealable freezer bag. Add chicken and marinate in refrigerator for 4 hours. Drain, discarding marinade.

Combine panko crumbs and paprika. Press chicken into panko mixture until coated. Arrange on a greased wire rack set in a baking sheet. Spray with cooking spray. Bake in a 450°F (230°C) oven for about 15 minutes until crisp and no longer pink inside.

Combine juice and brown sugar in a saucepan. Boil gently on medium for about 25 minutes until thickened to a syrup consistency.

Stir in rum and mustard. Serve with chicken. Serves 10.

1 serving: *148 Calories; 4.6 g Total Fat (3.1 g Mono, 0.5 g Poly, 0.7 g Sat); 20 mg Cholesterol; 16 g Carbohydrate; trace Fibre; 9 g Protein; 141 mg Sodium*

GARNISH
sprig of parsley

ABOUT PANKO
Panko is Japanese cuisine's version of the bread crumb. Unlike North American bread crumbs, panko tends to be flaky-looking. Panko comes in two forms, white and tan. White panko is derived from using crustless bread, while tan panko contains all parts of the bread. If it's unavailable at your local grocer's, you should be able to find it at an Asian market. For a subtle change to your other dishes, substitute panko where you would usually use regular bread crumbs.

These **refined** chicken fingers are paired with a **very-adult** coconut rum dip to ease your guests into contemplating the **finer things** life has to offer.

Savoury Shortbread Trio

Butter, room temperature	3/4 cup	175 mL
Icing (confectioner's) sugar	1/3 cup	75 mL
All-purpose flour	1 1/4 cups	300 mL
Salt	1/8 tsp.	0.5 mL
CHIVE, LEMON AND POPPY SEED SHORTBREAD		
Chopped fresh chives	2 tbsp.	30 mL
Grated lemon zest	1 tsp.	5 mL
Poppy seeds	1 tsp.	5 mL
PECAN, CURRY AND CILANTRO SHORTBREAD		
Chopped pecans, toasted (see How To, page 208)	1 tbsp.	15 mL
Finely chopped fresh cilantro	1 tsp.	5 mL
Madras curry paste	1 tsp.	5 mL
PINE NUT, BASIL AND PEPPER SHORTBREAD		
Chopped pine nuts, toasted (see How To, page 208)	2 tbsp.	30 mL
Finely chopped fresh basil	1 tbsp.	15 mL
Coarsely ground pepper	1/4 tsp.	1 mL

Cream butter and sugar. Stir in flour and salt until no dry flour remains. Divide into 3 equal portions.

Chive, Lemon And Poppy Seed Shortbread: Stir all 3 ingredients into 1 portion of dough.

Pecan, Curry And Cilantro Shortbread: Stir all 3 ingredients into 1 portion of dough.

Pine Nut, Basil And Pepper Shortbread: Stir all 3 ingredients into remaining portion of dough.

Roll each dough mixture into a 4 inch (10 cm) cylinder (see How To, below) and wrap individually with parchment paper. Chill for about 1 hour until firm. Cut into 1/4 inch (6 mm) thick slices and arrange on cookie sheets. Bake in a 300°F (150°C) oven for about 15 minutes until golden. Makes about 48 shortbread.

3 shortbread: 132 Calories; 10.0 g Total Fat (2.8 g Mono, 0.8 g Poly, 5.6 g Sat); 23 mg Cholesterol; 10 g Carbohydrate; trace Fibre; 1 g Protein; 90 mg Sodium

HOW TO FORM PERFECT CYLINDERS
To create uniform cylinders, first shape the dough into a log with your hands. Place the dough on the centre of a sheet of parchment (or waxed) paper, about 8 inches (20 cm) long, and fold the top half of the plastic wrap and parchment paper over the dough. Holding the edge of the parchment paper, use a pastry scraper or ruler to push the paper crease under the roll. The dough will form a perfect cylinder for easy and uniform slicing.

Perfectly suited for an evening of wine-tasting, these three tempting variations of savoury shortbread will melt in your mouth.

Fiery Plantain Chips
With Cocomango Dip

Large semi-ripe plantains, peeled	2	2
Cooking oil	2 tbsp.	30 mL
Chili oil	1 tbsp.	15 mL
Chili powder	1 tsp.	5 mL
Cayenne pepper	1/2 tsp.	2 mL
Finely chopped ripe mango	1/4 cup	60 mL
Sour cream	1/4 cup	60 mL
Coconut rum	2 tbsp.	30 mL
Medium unsweetened coconut, toasted (see How To, page 208)	2 tbsp.	30 mL
Granulated sugar	1 1/2 tsp.	7 mL
Lime juice	1 1/2 tsp.	7 mL
Ground allspice	1/8 tsp.	0.5 mL
Ground nutmeg, just a pinch		

Cut plantain at a sharp angle into 1/8 inch (3 mm) thick slices. Combine next 4 ingredients. Add plantain and toss gently until coated. Arrange in a single layer on 2 parchment paper-lined baking sheets. Bake in a 350°F (175°C) oven for 35 to 40 minutes, turning at halftime, until browned around edges. Let stand for 10 minutes.

Combine remaining 8 ingredients. Serve with chips. Serves 6.

1 serving: 166 Calories; 8.0 g Total Fat (3.8 g Mono, 1.2 g Poly, 2.6 g Sat); 4 mg Cholesterol; 22 g Carbohydrate; 2 g Fibre; 1 g Protein; 11 mg Sodium

---

GARNISH
fresh mango slices

ABOUT PLANTAINS
Plantains can usually be used at any sign of ripeness, but for this recipe you'll want to choose ones that are light yellow with a few black spots and no soft areas. Although they look like bananas, they are nowhere near as easy to peel. To peel, cut off the ends and run a sharp knife through the peel and down the inside curve. Do this three or four more times around the rest of the plantain. The strips should then peel away quite easily.

There are few finer **delights** than introducing your friends to a new taste **experience**—such as chili-infused plantains **tempered** with a cool and **soothing** coconut and mango dip.

Walnut Ginger Crisps

All-purpose flour	1 cup	250 mL
Minced crystallized ginger	1/3 cup	75 mL
Ground cardamom	1/2 tsp.	2 mL
Egg whites (large), room temperature (see Tip, below)	3	3
Brown sugar, packed	1/3 cup	75 mL
Walnut halves	1 1/4 cups	300 mL

Combine first 3 ingredients.

Beat egg whites and brown sugar until stiff peaks form (see How To, page 70). Fold in flour mixture until no dry flour remains.

Fold in walnuts and spread evenly in a greased 9 x 5 x 3 inch (22 x 12.5 x 7.5 cm) loaf pan, lined with parchment paper. Bake in a 350°F (175°C) oven for about 25 minutes until golden and firm. Transfer pan to a wire rack and let stand for 45 minutes. Remove the loaf from pan. Using a serrated knife, cut into 1/8 inch (3 mm) thick slices and arrange on a baking sheet. Bake in a 300°F (150°C) oven for about 15 minutes, turning at halftime, until dry and crisp. Transfer baking sheet to a wire rack and let stand until cool. Makes about 36 crisps.

1 crisp: 50 Calories; 2.3 g Total Fat (0.3 g Mono, 1.6 g Poly, 0.2 g Sat); 0 mg Cholesterol; 7 g Carbohydrate; trace Fibre; 1 g Protein; 7 mg Sodium

TIP
It is easiest to separate your eggs when they are cold, but always beat them at room temperature.

EXPERIMENT!
To add a delectable touch of sweetness, dip one end of each crisp in melted white chocolate.

Romance the **tantalizing** and **aromatic** **qualities** of cardamom and ginger in these refined crisps that are **well-suited** to serving with a **cheese** tray, custard, **mousse** or ice cream.

Halibut Bites
In Peppered Panko Crust

All-purpose flour	3 tbsp.	50 mL
Seasoned salt	1/2 tsp.	2 mL
Large egg	1	1
Lemon juice	1 tbsp.	15 mL
Panko bread crumbs	1 cup	250 mL
Coarsely ground pepper	1 tbsp.	15 mL
Halibut fillets (any small bones removed), cut into 1 inch (2.5 cm) pieces	3/4 lb.	340 g
Cooking oil	3 cups	750 mL
Coarse sea salt	1 tsp.	5 mL
Grated lemon zest	1 tsp.	5 mL

Combine flour and seasoned salt in a large resealable freezer bag.

Beat egg and lemon juice in a small shallow bowl.

Combine panko crumbs and pepper in a separate large resealable freezer bag.

Toss halibut in flour mixture until coated. Dip into egg mixture, then toss in crumb mixture until coated.

Heat cooking oil in a large frying pan on medium (see How To, page 124). Shallow-fry halibut for about 2 minutes, turning once, until golden. Transfer with a slotted spoon to a paper towel-lined plate to drain.

Sprinkle with sea salt and lemon zest. Makes about 24 bites.

1 bite: 60 Calories; 3.6 g Total Fat (2.0 g Mono, 1.0 g Poly, 0.3 g Sat); 12 mg Cholesterol; 3 g Carbohydrate; trace Fibre; 4 g Protein; 133 mg Sodium

---

GARNISH
lemon wedges

EXPERIMENT!
Halibut Bites are also great with a side of tartar sauce. Try making your own sauce by adding a little relish and chives to some lemon mayonnaise.

A welcome, yet unexpected offering at any **gathering**, these cubes of **pure-white halibut** are encased in a **peppery, crisp** golden crust. Your guests will **delight** in their **uniqueness**.

Shrimp Corn Cakes
With Lime Sauce

Large egg	1	1
Chopped cooked shrimp (peeled and deveined)	1 cup	250 mL
Finely chopped kernel corn	1/2 cup	125 mL
All-purpose flour	2 tbsp.	30 mL
Chopped fresh cilantro	2 tbsp.	30 mL
Yellow cornmeal	2 tbsp.	30 mL
Sour cream	1 tbsp.	15 mL
Seasoned salt	1/2 tsp.	2 mL
Butter	2 tbsp.	30 mL
Lime juice	2 tsp.	10 mL
Minced chipotle pepper in adobo sauce (see Tip, page 202)	1 1/2 tsp.	7 mL

Whisk egg until frothy. Stir in next 7 ingredients to form a thick batter.

Melt about 1 tbsp. (15 mL) butter in a large frying pan on medium. Drop 1 tbsp. (15 mL) portions of batter into pan. Cook for 1 to 2 minutes per side until golden. Transfer cakes to a serving platter and keep warm in a 200°F (95°C) oven. Repeat with remaining batter, adding butter between batches to prevent sticking.

Combine lime juice and chipotle pepper. Drizzle over corn cakes and serve immediately. Makes about 12 corn cakes.

1 corn cake: 60 Calories; 2.8 g Total Fat (0.8 g Mono, 0.3 g Poly, 1.5 g Sat); 58 mg Cholesterol; 4 g Carbohydrate; trace Fibre; 5 g Protein; 123 mg Sodium

HOW TO PIT AND SLICE AN AVOCADO

GARNISH
avocado slices
sour cream

Ever-popular **southwestern flavours** add a contemporary and **appetizing** twist. These **refreshing** and **delicious** cakes are best served with **margaritas,** beer or tequila.

Fresh. No matter what delicate morsel is artfully placed upon that verdant bed of lettuce, that single leaf of endive, that perfectly grilled asparagus, you know you're going to experience something crisp, clean and refreshing. But that's only one element in this gourmet interaction. How will the greens be contrasted, complemented or enhanced? Explore, and let your taste buds come alive.

On The Green

Glorious ways with leafy and vegetable greens

Almond Brie Croutons
On Apple-Dressed Spinach

Large egg, fork-beaten	1	1
Maple syrup	1 tbsp.	15 mL
Brie cheese round, cut into 6 wedges (see Tip, below)	7 1/2 oz.	200 g
All-purpose flour	1/4 cup	60 mL
Finely chopped sliced natural almonds	1 cup	250 mL
Maple syrup	2 tbsp.	30 mL
Olive oil	2 tbsp.	30 mL
White balsamic (or wine) vinegar	2 tbsp.	30 mL
Fresh spinach leaves, lightly packed	1 1/2 cups	375 mL
Unpeeled green apple, core removed and cut crosswise into thin rings	1	1

Combine egg and first amount of maple syrup.

Press cheese wedges into flour until coated. Dip into egg mixture, then press firmly into almonds until coated. Freeze for 45 minutes. Place wedges on a baking sheet. Bake in a 450°F (230°C) oven for about 7 minutes until almonds start to brown on edges and cheese starts to soften.

Combine next 3 ingredients in a bowl. Add spinach and apple and toss until coated. Spoon onto a serving plate, placing some of the apple rings over spinach. Arrange cheese wedges over top. Serves 6.

1 serving: 359 Calories; 27.2 g Total Fat (14.2 g Mono, 3.7 g Poly, 8.0 g Sat); 66 mg Cholesterol; 17 g Carbohydrate; 3 g Fibre; 14 g Protein; 248 mg Sodium

---

TIP
When working with softer cheeses like Brie, you can freeze them for 15 to 20 minutes to make cutting and portioning easier.

This **delicately** dressed spinach salad is **adorned** with decadent "croutons"—crusted in **almonds** and featuring a soft Brie centre. This **divine delicacy** embodies the word "heavenly."

Smoked Tuna And Wasabi Cream
In Endive Boats

Paper-thin English cucumber slices (with peel)	36	36
Rice vinegar	1 tbsp.	15 mL
Granulated sugar	1 tsp.	10 mL
Salt	1/4 tsp.	1 mL
Sour cream	2 tbsp.	30 mL
Grated lime zest	1 1/4 tsp.	6 mL
Wasabi paste	3/4 tsp.	4 mL
Medium Belgian endive leaves	12	12
Can of smoked light tuna slices, drained	4 1/2 oz.	120 g

Combine first 4 ingredients. Let stand for 10 minutes.

Combine next 3 ingredients.

Arrange endive on a serving plate. Arrange 3 overlapping cucumber slices on 1 end of each leaf. Top with a half slice of tuna. Spoon wasabi mixture over top. Makes 12 endive boats.

1 endive boat: *: 19 Calories; 0.6 g Total Fat (0.1 g Mono, 0.1 g Poly, 0.3 g Sat); 1 mg Cholesterol; 3 g Carbohydrate; 2 g Fibre; 1 g Protein; 60 mg Sodium*

GARNISH
salmon caviar

ABOUT SALMON CAVIAR
If you are worried about depleting fish resources, ease your mind. Salmon roe is a non-traditional type of caviar that comes from sustainable sources. Using it will leave the traditional sturgeon sources protected. As another alternative, tiny red caviar will provide a less assertive fish taste but will still maintain a nice, salty flavour.

Red-orange **pearls** of caviar provide a **glorious** garnish to the **artful display** of smoked tuna on an endive leaf. The **contrasting tastes** and textures meld beautifully in a **multi-faceted** encounter.

Seared Scallops Verde

Lime juice	3 tbsp.	50 mL
Olive oil	2 tbsp.	30 mL
Salt	1/8 tsp.	0.5 mL
Pepper	1/8 tsp.	0.5 mL
Large sea scallops	8	8
Chili powder, sprinkle		
Olive oil	1 tbsp.	15 mL
Tomatillo salsa (or salsa verde)	1/2 cup	125 mL
Small seedless watermelon triangles, about 1/2 inch (12 mm) thick	8	8

Combine first 4 ingredients. Add scallops and stir. Marinate for 15 minutes. Drain, discarding marinade.

Sprinkle chili powder over scallops. Heat second amount of olive oil in a frying pan on medium-high. Add scallops and sear for about 1 minute per side until scallops are just opaque.

Spoon small portions of salsa onto 8 small plates. Place watermelon triangles over salsa. Place scallops over watermelon and top with remaining salsa. Serves 8.

1 serving: 70 Calories; 3.6 g Total Fat (2.5 g Mono, 0.4 g Poly, 0.5 g Sat); 5 mg Cholesterol; 7 g Carbohydrate; trace Fibre; 3 g Protein; 102 mg Sodium

---

ABOUT SCALLOPS

Scallops range in colour from beige to creamy pink and should have a seawater smell to them. If scallops are white and odourless, they have most likely been soaked in a solution that plumps them up and increases their longevity. Scallops are notoriously easy to overcook, so it is very important to precisely follow recipe cooking times.

ABOUT SEARING

Searing is the process of cooking at a high temperature to give food an attractive crust. In this recipe you want to achieve the brown crust while cooking the scallops only long enough that they just lose their shiny, translucent appearance.

An **unpredicted** pairing of **succulent** chili-crusted **scallops** with the **tang** of a tomatillo salsa is made even more **momentous** with the addition of **fresh** watermelon.

Warm Ginger Chicken
Over Spinach

Dry sherry	1 tbsp.	15 mL
Soy sauce	1 tbsp.	15 mL
Sesame oil	1 tsp.	5 mL
Boneless, skinless chicken breast halves, cut into thin strips	1/2 lb.	225 g
Cooking oil	1 tsp.	5 mL
Thinly sliced fresh shiitake mushrooms, stems removed	1 cup	250 mL
Thinly sliced red pepper	1/2 cup	125 mL
Finely grated gingerroot	1 tbsp.	15 mL
Rice vinegar	3 tbsp.	50 mL
Cooking oil	2 tbsp.	30 mL
Sesame oil	1 tbsp.	15 mL
Soy sauce	1 tbsp.	15 mL
Baby spinach leaves, lightly packed	4 cups	1 L

Combine first 3 ingredients. Add chicken and stir. Let stand for 15 minutes.

Heat cooking oil in a frying pan on medium-high. Add chicken mixture and stir-fry for about 5 minutes until no longer pink. Transfer to a bowl.

Add next 3 ingredients to the same frying pan and stir-fry until mushrooms start to soften.

Stir in next 4 ingredients and chicken. Remove from heat and let stand for 5 minutes.

Arrange spinach on a serving plate. Spoon chicken mixture over top, drizzling with pan juices. Serve immediately (see Tip, below). Serves 4.

1 serving: 199 Calories; 13.6 g Total Fat (6.7 g Mono, 4.5 g Poly, 1.5 g Sat); 33 mg Cholesterol; 4 g Carbohydrate; 2 g Fibre; 15 g Protein; 455 mg Sodium

---

GARNISH
toasted sesame seeds

TIP
It is important that this salad be served immediately to prevent the spinach from becoming limp or wilted.

Sweet Asian flavours **accent** this **delicate**, miniature stir-fry set atop a **verdant**, leafy bed. Set the scene by serving this dish with **soothing jasmine tea** or warm sake.

Praline Pecans, Beets And Blue Cheese
On Baby Greens

Medium fresh beet, scrubbed clean	1	1
Butter	2 tsp.	10 mL
Brown sugar, lightly packed	1/4 cup	60 mL
Pecan halves	3/4 cup	175 mL
Orange juice	1/4 cup	60 mL
Chopped fresh chives	2 tbsp.	30 mL
Olive oil	2 tbsp.	30 mL
White wine vinegar	2 tbsp.	30 mL
Dijon mustard	1 tbsp.	15 mL
Pepper	1/8 tsp.	0.5 mL
Mixed baby greens, lightly packed	1 1/2 cups	375 mL
Crumbled blue (or goat) cheese	1/2 cup	125 mL

Microwave beet, covered, for about 4 minutes until tender. Let stand until cool. Peel and cut into 1/4 inch (6 mm) wedges (see Tip, below).

Heat and stir butter and brown sugar in a frying pan until sugar is dissolved. Stir in pecans. Spread on a baking sheet lined with greased foil. Bake in a 375°F (190°C) oven for about 8 minutes, stirring once, until browned. Transfer to cutting board. Let stand until cool, then chop.

Whisk next 6 ingredients together.

Arrange greens in the centre of a serving plate. Arrange beet wedges around greens. Sprinkle with cheese and pecans and drizzle with dressing. Serves 4.

1 serving: 350 Calories; 28.6 g Total Fat (14.5 g Mono, 5.4 g Poly, 6.0 g Sat); 18 mg Cholesterol; 21 g Carbohydrate; 3 g Fibre; 6 g Protein; 279 mg Sodium

TIP
It is advisable to wear gloves when cutting fresh beets to avoid staining your hands. It is also easier to peel beets after they have been microwaved or roasted—the skins will slip off quite easily.

ALTERNATIVE METHOD
Instead of microwaving your beet, you can roast it in the oven. Wrap the beet in foil and bake in a 375°F (190°C) oven for about 1 1/2 hours until tender. Remove and discard the foil and let the beet cool before peeling.

Vivid **beet** and candied pecans add a **distinguished essence** to blue cheese and **mixed greens**. With the addition of a citrus and Dijon dressing, the result is a virtual **kaleidoscope** of flavours.

Miso-Glazed Cod
On Ginger-Spiked Cucumbers

Paper-thin sliced English cucumber (with peel)	2 cups	500 mL
Paper-thin red onion slice, halved and separated	1	1
Brown sugar, packed	2 tbsp.	30 mL
Mirin	2 tbsp.	30 mL
Rice vinegar	2 tbsp.	30 mL
Finely grated gingerroot	1 tsp.	5 mL
Black sesame seeds	1 tsp.	5 mL
Sesame seeds	1 tsp.	5 mL
Cod fillets, any small bones removed (about 6 oz., 170 g, each)	2	2
Brown sugar, packed	3 tbsp.	50 mL
Mirin	3 tbsp.	50 mL
White miso	2 tbsp.	30 mL

Combine first 6 ingredients and marinate in refrigerator for 1 hour. Drain, discarding marinade. Arrange on a serving plate.

Sprinkle with sesame seeds.

Place cod fillets on a baking sheet. Microwave next 3 ingredients until brown sugar is dissolved and brush over fillets. Broil for 5 to 10 minutes until fish flakes easily when tested with a fork. Serve over cucumbers. Serves 4.

1 serving: 209 Calories; 1.8 g Total Fat (0.5 g Mono, 0.8 g Poly, 0.3 g Sat); 47 mg Cholesterol; 23 g Carbohydrate; 1 g Fibre; 21 g Protein; 301 mg Sodium

---

ABOUT MISO
Miso is a fermented soybean paste that is used in Japanese cooking. There are many varieties of miso with numerous colours and tastes, but the two most popular varieties in North America are white and red miso. White miso is actually yellowish in colour and has a sweet taste. Red miso is dark brown in colour and imparts a salty flavour. If not available from your grocer, it can be found at an Asian market.

ABOUT MIRIN
Mirin is a sweet Japanese cooking wine with a golden hue. If unavailable at your supermarket, try an Asian market.

Caramel-coloured glazed cod is set atop an Asian cucumber salad. The outcome is stylishly fresh and stimulating.

Ruby Chard

With Jerk Cornmeal Tofu "Croutons"

Olive oil	2 tbsp.	30 mL
Apple cider vinegar	1 tbsp.	15 mL
Jerk paste	1 tbsp	15 mL
Granulated sugar	1 tsp.	5 mL
Package of extra-firm tofu (5 x 3 inch, 12.5 x 7.5 cm, block), cut lengthwise into 4 slices	12 oz.	340 g
Yellow cornmeal	1/4 cup	60 mL
Olive oil	1 tbsp.	15 mL
Olive oil	1 tsp.	5 mL
Coarsely chopped ruby (or rainbow) chard, lightly packed	4 cups	1 L
Dried apricots, halved	1/4 cup	60 mL
Dark raisins	1/4 cup	60 mL

Whisk first 4 ingredients together. Pour over tofu, turning until coated. Marinate, covered, for 30 minutes. Remove tofu, reserving remaining marinade.

Press tofu into cornmeal until coated.

Heat second amount of olive oil in a frying pan on medium. Add tofu and cook until browned on both sides. Transfer to a plate and cover to keep warm. Wipe frying pan clean with a paper towel.

Heat third amount of olive oil in the same frying pan. Add remaining 3 ingredients with reserved marinade and cook, covered, for about 2 minutes until chard is wilted and stalks are tender-crisp. Transfer to a serving plate. Arrange tofu over top. Serves 4.

1 serving: 241 Calories; 13.1 g Total Fat (8.6 g Mono, 2.0 g Poly, 1.8 g Sat); 0 mg Cholesterol; 25 g Carbohydrate; 3 g Fibre; 8 g Protein; 348 mg Sodium

---

ABOUT RUBY CHARD
Ruby chard is a leafy member of the beet family. It has crinkly green leaves and bright reddish-purple stalks. Often it is prepared in the same manner as spinach. Choose chard with crisp stalks and tender, unblemished leaves. Store, wrapped in plastic, in the fridge for up to three days.

This **thrilling fusion** of Jamaican, Asian and southern
influences will **amuse** and **please** your guests.
Consider this small plate a **cuisine adventure**
with a very favourable outcome.

Salmon
With Herb Sabayon

Egg yolks (large)	4	4
Dry white wine	1/3 cup	75 mL
Lemon juice	2 tbsp.	30 mL
Granulated sugar	1 tbsp.	15 mL
Chopped fresh basil	1 tbsp.	15 mL
Chopped fresh oregano	1 tbsp.	15 mL
Chopped fresh thyme	1 tsp.	5 mL
Salmon fillet, skin removed	1/2 lb.	225 g
Olive oil	1/2 tsp.	2 mL
Salt, just a pinch		
Pepper, just a pinch		
Butter lettuce leaves	4	4

To make sabayon, whisk first 4 ingredients in a medium stainless steel bowl until frothy. Set over simmering water in a large saucepan so that the bottom of the bowl is not touching the water. Whisk for 1 to 2 minutes until mixture is thickened enough to leave a path on the back of a spoon when you run your finger through it (see How To, below).

Stir in next 3 ingredients.

Place salmon on a greased baking sheet. Drizzle with olive oil and sprinkle with salt and pepper. Broil for about 5 minutes until fish flakes easily when tested with a fork. Let stand for 2 minutes.

Arrange salmon over lettuce leaves on a serving plate. Serve with sabayon. Serves 4.

1 serving: 195 Calories; 11.6 g Total Fat (5.1 g Mono, 2.0 g Poly, 3.1 g Sat); 227 mg Cholesterol; 4 g Carbohydrate; trace Fibre; 14 g Protein; 35 mg Sodium

HOW TO PLACE THE BOWL AND CHECK FOR THICKNESS

GARNISH
lemon peel

Subtle wine essence, **aromatic** lemon and **delicate herb** notes surround a succulent piece of broiled salmon—this small plate is **exquisite** whether served **hot** or **cold**.

Citrus-Glazed Lobster And Fennel

Orange juice	1 cup	250 mL
Granulated sugar	2 tbsp.	30 mL
Sesame oil	2 tsp.	10 mL
Thinly sliced fennel bulb (white part only)	2 cups	500 mL
Garlic cloves, minced	2	2
Poppy seeds, sprinkle		
Sesame oil	2 tsp.	10 mL
Raw lobster tails, meat removed (see How To, below), cut into 6 pieces each	2	2
Sea salt, sprinkle		

Combine orange juice and sugar in a saucepan. Boil gently on medium for about 20 minutes, stirring occasionally, until reduced to about 1/4 cup (60 mL).

Heat first amount of sesame oil in a frying pan on medium. Add fennel and garlic and cook for about 5 minutes until fennel is tender-crisp. Transfer to a serving plate.

Drizzle with 1 tbsp. (15 mL) juice reduction and sprinkle with poppy seeds.

Heat second amount of sesame oil. Add lobster and sprinkle with sea salt. Cook for about 3 minutes until lobster is opaque and lightly browned. Arrange over fennel, drizzling with remaining juice reduction. Serves 4.

1 serving: 196 Calories; 5.3 g Total Fat (1.9 g Mono, 1.9 g Poly, 0.7 g Sat); 34 mg Cholesterol; 27 g Carbohydrate; 6 g Fibre; 12 g Protein; 275 mg Sodium

---

GARNISH
sprigs of fresh parsley

HOW TO REMOVE LOBSTER MEAT
To remove the lobster meat from the tail, firmly grasp the tail and snap off the flipper portion. Use a fork to press up from the flipper end and push the meat out of the top of the shell.

A simple dressing of **orange reduction** brings out the natural sweetness of the **lobster**. This dish will impress those guests with even the most adventurous palates.

Chili Squid
On Peas And Peppers

Squid tubes (about 4 inches, 10 cm, each)	6	6
Soy sauce	1 tbsp.	15 mL
Dried crushed chilies	1/2 tsp.	2 mL
Cooking oil	2 tsp.	10 mL
Thinly sliced red pepper	1 cup	250 mL
Sugar snap peas	1/2 lb.	225 g
Garlic cloves, minced	2	2
Sweet chili sauce	1/3 cup	75 mL
Chili paste (sambal oelek)	1/4 tsp.	1 mL
Seasoned salt	1/2 tsp.	2 mL
Cooking oil	2 tsp.	10 mL

Cut squid tubes lengthwise to open flat. Score inside surface in a crosshatch pattern. Cut each piece in half and transfer to a bowl. Add soy sauce and chilies and stir. Chill, covered, for 30 minutes.

Heat a frying pan on medium-high until very hot. Add cooking oil. Add next 3 ingredients and stir-fry for about 1 minute until fragrant.

Add next 3 ingredients and stir-fry for about 2 minutes until vegetables are tender-crisp. Transfer to a serving plate.

Add second amount of cooking oil to the same frying pan. Add squid mixture and stir-fry for about 1 minute until squid curls. Arrange over vegetables, drizzling with pan juices. Serves 4.

1 serving: 143 Calories; 5.1 g Total Fat (2.7 g Mono, 1.6 g Poly, 0.5 g Sat); 66 mg Cholesterol; 17 g Carbohydrate; 2 g Fibre; 7 g Protein; 591 mg Sodium

TIP
Like most seafood, squid can become unpalatable when overcooked. Follow the cooking instructions precisely.

One of the **joys of cooking** is boldly stepping into new culinary **territory**. Buying and preparing an unfamiliar ingredient sends **delightful shivers** down the spine. Easily managed, this spicy squid delivers **beautiful results**.

Herb Olive Feta Mélange
Over Grilled Asparagus

Fresh asparagus, trimmed of tough ends	1 lb.	454 g
Olive oil	1 tbsp.	15 mL
Salt, sprinkle		
Pepper, sprinkle		
Diced feta cheese	1/3 cup	75 mL
Large pitted green olives	1/3 cup	75 mL
Large pitted kalamata olives	1/3 cup	75 mL
Chopped fresh basil	1 tbsp.	15 mL
Chopped fresh oregano	1 tbsp.	15 mL
Chopped fresh rosemary	1 tsp.	5 mL
Roasted garlic olive oil	2 tbsp.	30 mL

Toss asparagus in olive oil and sprinkle with salt and pepper. Cook on a greased grill on medium for about 5 minutes, turning occasionally, until browned. Arrange on a serving platter.

Sprinkle with next 6 ingredients. Drizzle with garlic olive oil. Serves 6.

1 serving: 132 Calories; 11.5 g Total Fat (7.5 g Mono, 1.5 g Poly, 2.4 g Sat); 8 mg Cholesterol; 5 g Carbohydrate; 2 g Fibre; 3 g Protein; 377 mg Sodium

---

GARNISH
lemon peel
freshly ground black pepper

HOW TO PIT OLIVES
Although there are olive pitters on the market, pitting by hand is easy. First, you must break the skin so it releases the pit. Do this by rolling and squeezing between your fingers. Or you can press down on the olive with a broad-bladed knife. Once the skin is broken, you should easily be able to remove the pit with your fingers or tweezers.

ALTERNATIVE METHOD
Let the olives and cheese marinate in the herbs and olive oil overnight—this will allow the herb flavours to diffuse throughout the mixture.

A topping of **herbs,** **olives and feta** provides a **complex** contrast to the simple, fresh **flavour** of grilled asparagus.

Caramel Pork Tenderloin
On Bok Choy

Water	1 cup	250 mL
Granulated sugar	2/3 cup	150 mL
Soy sauce	6 tbsp.	100 mL
Thai hot chili peppers, finely chopped (see Tip, below)	3	3
Pork tenderloin, trimmed of fat	3/4 lb.	340 g
Sesame oil	1 tsp.	5 mL
Seasoned salt	1/4 tsp.	1 mL
Baby bok choy, cut in half	2 cups	500 mL

Heat and stir water and sugar in a small saucepan on medium until sugar is dissolved. Boil gently for about 12 minutes, brushing side of pan with a wet pastry brush (see How To, below), until a medium brown colour. Stir in soy sauce and chili peppers.

Place pork on a greased wire rack set in a foil-lined baking sheet. Brush with sesame oil and sprinkle with salt. Bake in a 475°F (240°C) oven for 20 minutes. Brush with 2 tbsp. (30 mL) caramel mixture. Broil for about 2 minutes until internal temperature of pork reaches 160°F (70°C) or desired doneness. Cover with foil and let stand for 10 minutes. Cut into 1/4 inch (6 mm) thick slices.

Cook bok choy in boiling water for about 1 minute until slightly wilted. Drain. Rinse with cold water. Drain well. Serve with pork and remaining caramel mixture. Serves 6.

1 serving: 178 Calories; 2.7 g Total Fat (0.8 g Mono, 0.2 g Poly, 0.7 g Sat); 34 mg Cholesterol; 27 g Carbohydrate; 1 g Fibre; 13 g Protein; 1417 mg Sodium

HOW TO MAKE CARAMEL SAUCE
Brushing the side of the saucepan with a wet pastry brush helps to dissolve any sugar crystals.

TIP
Hot peppers contain capsaicin in the seeds and ribs, so removing them will reduce the amount of heat. When handling hot peppers, avoid touching your eyes. Be sure to wash your hands well afterwards.

With an **exciting** variety of tastes and textures, from **tender pork** to crisp, fresh bok choy with a sweet and **spicy caramel** sauce, this dish is both **surprising** and impressive.

Alluring. The secret of these small plates is hidden on the inside. Sometimes there's a telltale glimpse—perhaps a familiar hue, just peeking out—the rich green of fresh herbs or the lively orange of mango. Maybe it's the aroma that's sending signals to your brain—the beckoning fragrance of ginger, pesto, curry or parmesan—hinting at an exquisite taste that's at first elusive, then familiar. Whatever it is, you're curious. And discovering what's inside is as simple as taking a bite.

Rolled Up & Tucked In

Tenderly wrapped or filled temptations

Feta And Herb Eggplant Rolls

Asian eggplants, ends trimmed	3	3
Olive oil	2 tbsp.	30 mL
Salt, sprinkle		
Pepper, sprinkle		
Canned roasted whole red peppers, drained, blotted dry, cut into 4 strips each	3	3
Crumbled feta cheese	1/2 cup	125 mL
Herb and garlic cream cheese	1/4 cup	60 mL
Chopped fresh basil	3 tbsp.	50 mL
Arugula leaves	36	36
Wooden cocktail picks	12	12
Balsamic vinegar	2 tbsp.	30 mL

Cut eggplants lengthwise into 6 slices each, about 1/4 inch (6 mm) thick. Discard outside slices. Brush both sides of slices with olive oil and sprinkle with salt and pepper. Cook on a greased grill on medium for about 5 minutes until browned. Let stand until cool.

Place 1 strip of red pepper on each eggplant slice.

Combine next 3 ingredients and spread over red pepper. Arrange arugula leaves over top. Roll up eggplant slices to enclose filling, securing with wooden picks. Arrange rolls, seam-side down, on a serving plate.

Brush with vinegar. Serve at room temperature. Makes 12 rolls.

1 roll: 83 Calories; 5.6 g Total Fat (2.0 g Mono, 0.3 g Poly, 2.5 g Sat); 11 mg Cholesterol; 5 g Carbohydrate; 1 g Fibre; 2 g Protein; 222 mg Sodium

---

HOW TO SALT EGGPLANT
If using an eggplant variety that isn't Asian, you may want to salt it. This reduces its natural bitter flavour and make it less likely to absorb too much oil. Simply cut the eggplant as directed and generously sprinkle with salt. Set aside for an hour and then thoroughly rinse with water. Squeeze out any excess water and blot until completely dry.

ALTERNATIVE METHOD
If you prefer to forgo the grill, you can bake your eggplant slices in a 375°F (190°C) oven for 15 to 20 minutes until lightly browned.

The rich **royal purple** skin of an Asian eggplant
lends an intriguing hue to this **sophisticated** roll.
The **fresh flavours** with **smoky accents**
and a hint of tang are bound to **tantalize**.

Curried Chicken Samosa Strudel

Cooking oil	2 tsp.	10 mL
Minced onion	1 1/2 cups	375 mL
Madras curry paste	2 tbsp.	30 mL
Garlic cloves, minced	2	2
Canned chickpeas (garbanzo beans), rinsed and drained, mashed	1 cup	250 mL
Chopped cooked chicken breast	1 cup	250 mL
Frozen peas	1/2 cup	125 mL
Grated carrot	1/2 cup	125 mL
Phyllo pastry sheets, thawed according to package directions	8	8
Unsalted butter, melted	1/4 cup	60 mL

Heat cooking oil in a frying pan on medium. Add next 3 ingredients and cook until onion starts to soften. Let stand until cool.

Stir in next 4 ingredients.

Layer 4 sheets of phyllo pastry, lightly brushing each layer with melted butter. Keep remaining phyllo covered with a damp towel to prevent drying. Spread half of chicken mixture along bottom of sheet, leaving a 1 1/2 inch (3.8 cm) edge on each side. Fold in sides and roll up from bottom to enclose. Place, seam-side down, on an ungreased baking sheet. Brush with butter. Cut several small vents on top to allow steam to escape. Repeat. Bake in a 400°F (205°C) oven for about 20 minutes until golden. With a serrated knife, cut strudels diagonally into 7 slices each. Makes 14 slices.

1 slice: 155 Calories; 6.2 g Total Fat (1.9 g Mono, 0.9 g Poly, 2.6 g Sat); 17 mg Cholesterol; 18 g Carbohydrate; 2 g Fibre; 7 g Protein; 148 mg Sodium

HOW TO ROLL STRUDEL

The crisp, delicate and **flaky texture** of **phyllo pastry** heightens the sensation of biting into these **mildly spiced** strudels.

Shrimp Mango Summer Rolls
With Cool Herbs And Chili Heat

Rice vermicelli	2 oz.	57 g
Chopped fresh mint	2 tbsp.	30 mL
Lime juice	2 tbsp.	30 mL
Sweet chili sauce	2 tbsp.	30 mL
Fish sauce	2 tsp.	10 mL
Rice paper rounds (7 inch, 18 cm, diameter)	6	6
Fresh cilantro leaves	12	12
Cooked medium shrimp (peeled and deveined), halved lengthwise	6	6
Mango slices, 1/8 inch (3 mm) thick (see Tip, below)	6	6

Cover vermicelli with boiling water. Let stand until just tender. Drain. Rinse with cold water, draining well. Add next 4 ingredients and toss well.

Place 1 rice paper round in a shallow bowl of hot water until just softened (see How To, below). Place on a clean tea towel. Place 2 cilantro leaves in the centre of the rice paper and 2 shrimp halves over top. Cover with a mango slice. Spoon about 3 tbsp. (50 mL) vermicelli mixture over top. Fold in sides and roll up tightly from bottom to enclose. Repeat. Serve with sweet chili sauce. Makes 6 rolls.

1 roll: 104 Calories; 0.2 g Total Fat (trace Mono, trace Poly, 0.1 g Sat); 11 mg Cholesterol; 22 g Carbohydrate; trace Fibre; 3 g Protein; 525 mg Sodium

---

TIP
If fresh mango isn't available, drained, canned mango can be substituted. The texture will be softer but the overall taste won't be compromised.

HOW TO WORK WITH RICE PAPER
In order to become pliable, rice paper must be softened in water. Thicker rice paper (as used in this recipe) requires hotter water whereas the thinner varieties can be softened in cooler water. If working with hot water, make sure to change it as it cools. Always soften one sheet at a time, quickly and evenly. If the rice paper becomes too soft, it may become sticky and hard to work with.

A touch of **chili heat** mingles with the cool crispness of **mint** and **cilantro** in these rolls that are filled with everything light, cool and **refreshing**.

Ginger Chicken Flowers

Lean ground chicken	6 oz.	170 g
Finely chopped green onion	1 tbsp.	15 mL
Finely grated carrot	1 tbsp.	15 mL
Minced red pepper	1 tbsp.	15 mL
Oyster sauce	2 tsp.	10 mL
Cornstarch	1 tsp.	5 mL
Finely grated gingerroot	1 tsp.	5 mL
Garlic clove, minced	1	1
Soy sauce	1 tsp.	5 mL
Round dumpling wrappers	8	8
Water		
Suey choy (Chinese cabbage) leaves	2	2
Hoisin sauce	1 tbsp.	15 mL
Water	1 tbsp.	15 mL

Combine first 9 ingredients.

Spoon chicken mixture onto centres of dumpling wrappers. Dampen edges with water. Gather up edges around filling, leaving tops open. Tap dumplings gently on work surface to flatten bottoms slightly.

Line bottom of a large bamboo steamer with suey choy leaves. Arrange dumplings so they do not touch each other or the sides of the steamer. Place steamer on a rack set over simmering water in a wok or Dutch oven. Cook, covered, for about 15 minutes until filling is no longer pink and temperature reaches 175°F (80°C).

Combine hoisin sauce and water and drizzle over dumplings. Makes 8 dumplings.

1 dumpling: 72 Calories; 3.1 g Total Fat (trace Mono, 0.1 g Poly, trace Sat); 1 mg Cholesterol; 6 g Carbohydrate; trace Fibre; 5 g Protein; 133 mg Sodium

---

ALTERNATIVE METHOD
If you don't have a bamboo steamer, arrange dumplings in a parchment paper-lined 9 x 9 inch (22 x 22 cm) baking pan, making sure they do not touch the sides of the pan or each other. Place a wire rack in the bottom of a roasting pan, and pour in water until 1 inch (2.5 cm) deep. Bring to a boil on the stovetop, then set the baking pan on the wire rack. Steam, covered, for about 15 minutes until the filling is no longer pink and temperature reaches 175°F (80°C).

Food becomes art when these delicate, **flower-inspired**, open dumplings **bloom**. Reminiscent of dim sum fare but far more visually stimulating, these beauties are certain to spark conversation.

Arugula Pesto Ravioli
With Browned Butter Pine Nuts

Fresh lasagna sheets (6 x 8 inches, 15 x 20 cm, each)	3	3
Arugula leaves, lightly packed	1 cup	250 mL
Pecan halves, toasted (see How To, page 208)	1/2 cup	125 mL
Basil pesto	1/3 cup	75 mL
Grated Asiago cheese	1/4 cup	60 mL
Butter	1/4 cup	60 mL
Pine nuts	3 tbsp.	50 mL
Chopped fresh parsley	2 tsp.	10 mL
Grated lemon zest	1 tsp.	5 mL

Cook lasagna sheets in boiling salted water for about 5 minutes until softened. Drain. Rinse with cold water, draining well.

In a blender or food processor, process next 3 ingredients until smooth. Stir in cheese. Spread 1/4 of arugula mixture over 1 lasagna sheet in a greased pan. Repeat layers, spreading remaining arugula mixture over top. Cut into 8 rectangles.

Melt butter in a frying pan on medium. Add pine nuts and cook until butter is browned. Drizzle over pasta rectangles. Bake, covered, in a 400°F (205°C) oven for about 15 minutes until heated through. Transfer to a serving plate.

Sprinkle with parsley and lemon zest. Makes 8 ravioli.

1 ravioli: 251 Calories; 19.4 g Total Fat (5.2 g Mono, 2.6 g Poly, 6 g Sat); 21 mg Cholesterol; 15 g Carbohydrate; 2 g Fibre; 6 g Protein; 164 mg Sodium

ABOUT ARUGULA
Arugula, also known as "rocket" in Britain and "rucola" in Italy, is a salad green with a lively peppery zing—in some cases it can be quite hot. Because of its vivid flavour, it is rarely served alone. Often it is mixed with other less-distinctly flavoured greens or is used as an accent piece for milder ingredients. In Italy, it is often served salad-style, with thick shavings of the popular Grana Padano cheese.

This deconstructed, highly **captivating** version of ravioli eliminates the hard labour yet yields a vision that **stimulates** the senses. With an **inspired combination** of flavours, the end result is a revelatory **experience**.

Mushroom Risotto Balls

Cooking oil	1 tsp.	5 mL
Finely chopped white mushrooms	1 cup	250 mL
Minced onion	1/2 cup	125 mL
Arborio rice	1/2 cup	125 mL
Dry white wine	1/4 cup	60 mL
Hot prepared vegetable broth	1 1/3 cups	325 mL
Pepper	1/4 tsp.	1 mL
Grated Parmesan cheese	1/4 cup	60 mL
Grated lemon zest	1/2 tsp.	2 mL
Asiago cheese cubes (1/2 inch, 12 mm)	12	12
All-purpose flour	2 tbsp.	30 mL
Cooking oil	3 cups	750 mL
Prepared rosé pasta sauce, warmed	1/2 cup	125 mL

Heat cooking oil in a saucepan on medium. Add mushrooms and onion and cook until softened. Add rice. Heat and stir for 30 seconds.

Add wine. Cook until wine is almost all evaporated. Stir in hot broth and pepper. Bring to a boil. Simmer, covered, on medium-low for about 15 minutes, without stirring, until rice is tender and liquid is absorbed.

Stir in Parmesan cheese and lemon zest. Spoon 2 tbsp. (30 mL) portions of risotto mixture onto a waxed paper-lined basheet. Let stand for 5 minutes to cool.

Place 1 Asiago cheese cube on each risotto mound. With wet hands, roll into balls, enclosing cheese. Lightly toss in flour.

Heat cooking oil in a large frying pan on medium-high (see How To, below). Shallow-fry risotto balls for 2 to 3 minutes, turning occasionally, until golden and heated through. Transfer to a paper towel-lined plate. Let stand for 2 minutes.

Drizzle pasta sauce on a serving plate. Arrange risotto balls over sauce. Makes about 12 risotto balls.

1 risotto ball: 105 Calories; 6.9 g Total Fat (1.1 g Mono, 0.5 g Poly, 3.4 g Sat); 16 mg Cholesterol; 5 g Carbohydrate; trace Fibre; 5 g Protein; 300 mg Sodium

---

GARNISH
sprigs of fresh parsley

HOW TO TEST OIL TEMPERATURE
Keep your fried foods crisp, rather than greasy, with properly heated oil that has reached 350 – 375°F (170 – 190°C).
The easiest way to test the temperature is to use a deep-fry thermometer. If you don't have a thermometer, try either of the following:

- Insert the tip of a wooden spoon. If the oil around it bubbles, the temperature is right.
- Toss in a small piece of bread. If it sizzles and turns brown within 1 minute, the oil is ready.

Inspired by the Italian taste sensation *arancini*
(food with a crisp outside and a soft, cheesy centre),
a **delectable treasure** of creamy Asiago is neatly tucked into
tempting, golden mushroom risotto balls.

Crispy Jerk Chicken Rolls

Cooking oil	1 tsp.	5 mL
Chopped onion	1 cup	250 mL
Grated carrot	1 cup	250 mL
Chopped pickled jalapeño pepper	1 tbsp.	15 mL
Jerk paste	1 1/4 tsp.	6 mL
Garlic clove, minced	1	1
Ground allspice	1/8 tsp.	0.5 mL
Chopped cooked chicken	1 cup	250 mL
Plain yogurt	2 tbsp.	30 mL
Spring roll wrappers (6 inch, 15 cm, square)	8	8
Egg white (large)	1	1
Water	1 tbsp.	15 mL
Cooking oil	3 cups	750 mL

Heat cooking oil in a frying pan on medium. Add next 6 ingredients and cook for about 10 minutes until onion is softened.

Stir in chicken and yogurt.

Arrange wrappers on work surface. Place about 1/4 cup (60 mL) chicken mixture near bottom right corner. Fold corner up and over filling, folding in sides. Dampen edges with a mixture of egg white and water. Roll to opposite corner and press to seal. Repeat.

Heat cooking oil in a large frying pan on medium-high (see How To, page 124). Shallow-fry 2 or 3 rolls at a time, turning often, until golden. Transfer to a paper towel-lined plate. Makes 8 rolls.

1 roll: 150 Calories; 5.1 g Total Fat (2.6 g Mono, 1.3 g Poly, 0.6 g Sat); 16 mg Cholesterol; 18 g Carbohydrate; 1 g Fibre; 9 g Protein; 227 mg Sodium

---

GARNISH
sliced jalapeño

EXPERIMENT!
Design your own jerk seasoning by playing around with varying amounts of the following spices: onion salt or flakes, thyme, cinnamon, cloves, allspice, ginger, garlic and cayenne. When you have achieved the right proportions, store in a plastic baggie so it's at the ready. Sprinkle on meat before barbecuing or make a simple dip by adding a small amount to sweet-and-sour sauce.

Indulge your guests with the **crisp, fried** fare that is so enjoyed at get-togethers—just make yours a **cut above** the rest with the Jamaican flair of **spicy jerk** chicken.

Parmesan Cones
With White Bean Mousse

Grated fresh Parmesan cheese (see Tip, below)	3/4 cup	175 mL
Pepper	1/4 tsp.	1 mL
Canned white kidney beans, rinsed and drained	1 cup	250 mL
Basil pesto	1 tbsp.	15 mL
Lemon juice	2 tsp.	10 mL
Olive oil	2 tsp.	10 mL

Cut two 3 1/2 inch (9 cm) diameter circles from heavy paper. Shape into cones and tape or staple securely. Place a sheet of parchment paper on a baking sheet (see Tip, below). Trace two 3 1/2 inch (9 cm) diameter circles, about 3 inches (7.5 cm) apart. Turn paper over. Combine cheese and pepper and spread about 1 tbsp. (15 mL) cheese mixture over each circle. Bake in a 350°F (175°C) oven for about 5 minutes until melted and golden. Let stand for 1 minute. Transfer cheese round to a plate. Immediately place 1 paper cone on cheese and roll around cone. Repeat with second cheese round and cone. Let stand until cool. Wipe parchment paper to remove any crumbs. Repeat.

In a blender or food processor, process remaining 4 ingredients until smooth. Spoon into a small freezer bag with a small piece snipped off 1 corner. Pipe into cones. Serve immediately. Makes about 10 cones.

1 cone: 71 Calories; 4.1 g Total Fat (1.3 g Mono, 0.1 g Poly, 1.7 g Sat); 6 mg Cholesterol; 4 g Carbohydrate; 1 g Fibre; 5 g Protein; 161 mg Sodium

GARNISH
sprigs of fresh basil

TIP
Don't cheat yourself by using powdered Parmesan. Grate the fresh stuff for truly magnificent flavour and perfect results.

TIP
Have two separate baking sheets at the ready, each with their own parchment paper with circles drawn on, so you can put the second one in the oven while the first one cools.

Although **reminiscent** of a favourite sweet treat, the eyes will play tricks on the **taste buds** when your guests bite into these rich, **savoury** cones. The interplay of Parmesan, basil and lemon is delightfully **unexpected**.

Prosciutto Arugula Herb Wraps

Milk	1 cup	250 mL
Large eggs	2	2
Butter, melted	1 1/2 tbsp.	25 mL
Chopped fresh basil	1 tbsp.	15 mL
Chopped fresh oregano	1 tbsp.	15 mL
Chopped fresh thyme	2 tsp.	10 mL
Salt	1/2 tsp.	2 mL
All-purpose flour	1/2 cup	125 mL
Cooking oil	1 tbsp.	15 mL
Chopped arugula leaves, lightly packed	1 1/2 cups	375 mL
Chopped prosciutto ham	2/3 cup	150 mL
Sour cream	1/3 cup	75 mL

In a blender or food processor, process first 7 ingredients. Transfer to a bowl. Whisk in flour until smooth.

Heat 1/4 tsp. (1 mL) cooking oil in a small frying pan on medium. Pour about 2 tbsp. (30 mL) batter into pan. Immediately tilt and swirl pan to ensure bottom is covered. Cook for about 1 minute until brown spots appear. Turn over. Cook until golden. Transfer to a plate. Repeat with remaining batter, adding and heating cooking oil between batches to prevent sticking.

Combine remaining 3 ingredients. Spoon about 2 tbsp. (30 mL) along centre of each wrapper. Fold in sides and roll up from bottom to enclose. Place, seam-side down, on a serving plate. Makes about 12 rolls.

1 roll: 101 Calories; 6.1 g Total Fat (1.8 g Mono, 0.6 g Poly, 2.5 g Sat); 49 mg Cholesterol; 6 g Carbohydrate; trace Fibre; 6 g Protein; 474 mg Sodium

---

HOW TO MAKE CRÈME FRAICHE
Enhance this recipe with dollops of your own crème fraiche. Simply add 3 tbsp. (50 mL) of buttermilk to 1 cup (250 mL) of whipping cream. Let stand at room temperature, covered, overnight. Chill for at least 8 hours before serving.

Worlds **collide** with this French and Italian-inspired delicacy. Thin little pancakes are **infused** with herbs and **wrapped** around peppery arugula and and **salty** prosciutto.

Seta Antojitos Especial

Olive oil	1 tbsp.	15 mL
Chopped portobello mushrooms	4 cups	1 L
Chopped leek (white part only)	1/2 cup	125 mL
Salt	1/4 tsp.	1 mL
Pepper	1/4 tsp.	1 mL
Madeira	2 tbsp.	30 mL
Chopped fresh thyme	1 1/2 tsp.	7 mL
Grated havarti cheese	1 1/2 cups	375 mL
Flour tortillas (9 inch, 22 cm, diameter)	2	2

Heat olive oil in a large frying pan on medium-high. Add next 4 ingredients and cook until mushrooms are browned and liquid is all evaporated.

Add Madeira and thyme and cook until wine is all evaporated. Remove from heat.

Stir in cheese. Spread over tortillas, leaving a 1/2 inch (12 mm) border. Roll up to enclose. Place, seam-side down, on a greased baking sheet. Bake in a 400°F (205°C) oven until browned and cheese is melted. Let stand for 2 minutes. Trim ends and cut diagonally into 5 slices each. Makes 10 slices.

1 slice: 199 Calories; 14.4 g Total Fat (1.0 g Mono, 0.1 g Poly, 8.9 g Sat); 30 mg Cholesterol; 7 g Carbohydrate; 1 g Fibre; 7 g Protein; 306 mg Sodium

---

GARNISH
sprigs of fresh thyme

ABOUT MADEIRA
Madeira hails from the island of the same name and is considered a fortified wine. There are four different kinds of Madeira, each based on the variety of grape used—which should be clearly displayed on the label. Malmsey is considered to be sweetest; Bual is of medium sweetness; Verdelho is medium dry; and Sercial is very dry. Madeira goes well with cheese and is best imbibed as an aperitif or dessert wine. It is traditionally served in a small, thin, port-style glass.

This tortilla wrap **surprises**.
Madiera and portobello add a **richness**
and **body** that completely **satisfies**.

Smoked Salmon Rice Rolls

Mixed baby greens	1 cup	250 mL
Julienned smoked salmon slices	6 oz.	170 g
(see How To, page 204)		
Julienned English cucumber	1/2 cup	125 mL
(see How To, 204)		
Enoki mushrooms	3 oz.	85 g
Grated carrot	1/3 cup	75 mL
Julienned green onion	1/4 cup	60 mL
(see How To, page 204)		
Sprigs of fresh dill, stems removed	6	6
Rice paper rounds (9 inch, 22 cm, diameter)	6	6
Black sesame seeds	1 tsp.	5 mL
Ponzu sauce (see Tip, below)	1/3 cup	75 mL

Divide each of the first 7 ingredients into 6 equal portions.

Place 1 rice paper round in a shallow bowl of hot water until just softened (see How To, page 118). Place on a clean tea towel. Arrange 1 portion of filling along centre of rice paper. Fold in sides and roll up tightly from bottom to enclose. Place, seam-side down, on a serving plate. Repeat.

Sprinkle sesame seeds over rolls. Serve with ponzu sauce. Makes 6 rolls.

1 roll with 2 1/2 tsp. (12 mL) sauce: 382 Calories; 2.1 g Total Fat (0.7 g Mono, 0.4 g Poly, 0.8 g Sat); 7 mg Cholesterol; 78 g Carbohydrate; 1 g Fibre; 12 g Protein; 1815 mg Sodium

---

TIP
If you can't find ponzu sauce, simply add a little lemon juice to regular soy sauce.

ABOUT ENOKI MUSHROOMS
Enoki mushrooms have a delicate flavour and an unexpected crunchiness. With tiny caps and long thin stems, they are usually found in the produce section in sealed bundles. They last up to two weeks sealed, but must be used immediately if opened. They can be enjoyed fresh and should only ever be lightly cooked. Overcooking will make them stringy and tough.

Smoked salmon adds extra dimension
to this special salad roll. The rich, salty fish and the cool,
fresh vegetables are balanced in Zen-like proportion.

Precise. When cooking with sharp sticks, you have to make decisions wisely. Senses will be on overdrive. This is food that will be touched as well as tasted. Take a stab at Pork Souvlaki With Red Pepper Yogurt or Leek-Wrapped Ginger Scallops With Soy Glaze. But venture carefully. You're creating a very special lineup: flavour…spiked.

Skewered

Clever queues of delectable bites

Dukkah Beef Skewers
With Wine Reduction

Balsamic vinegar	1/4 cup	60 mL
Dry red wine	1/4 cup	60 mL
Liquid honey	1/4 cup	60 mL
Hazelnuts (filberts)	14	14
Sesame seeds	2 tsp.	10 mL
Coriander seed	1 tsp.	5 mL
Cumin seed	1 tsp.	5 mL
Grated Reggiano Parmigiano cheese	2 tbsp.	30 mL
Coarsely ground pepper	1/4 tsp.	1 mL
Olive oil	2 tbsp.	30 mL
Dijon mustard	1 tbsp.	15 mL
Beef strip loin steak, cut into 1/4 inch (6 mm) slices	3/4 lb.	340 g
Bamboo skewers (8 inches, 20 cm, each), soaked in water for 10 minutes	16	16

Combine first 3 ingredients in a saucepan. Boil gently on medium for about 7 minutes until reduced by half.

Heat and stir next 4 ingredients in a frying pan on medium until toasted and fragrant. Let stand until cool. Transfer to a blender or food processor and process until coarsely ground.

Combine mixture with cheese and pepper on a plate.

Combine olive oil and mustard. Add beef and stir. Thread onto skewers and press into cheese mixture until coated. Cook on a greased grill on medium-high for 1 to 2 minutes per side until meat reaches desired doneness. Drizzle half of wine mixture over top. Serve immediately with remaining wine mixture. Makes 16 skewers.

1 skewer with 1/2 tsp. (2 mL) wine reduction: 98 Calories; 6.0 g Total Fat (3.3 g Mono, 0.5 g Poly, 1.7 g Sat); 14 mg Cholesterol; 5 g Carbohydrate; trace Fibre; 5 g Protein; 40 mg Sodium

ABOUT DUKKAH
Dukkah is a traditional Middle Eastern spice mix that lends flavour and texture to even the most basic dishes. Although the ingredients vary from cook to cook, they often include sesame seeds, hazelnuts, pistachios and spices native to the local area.

IMBIBE!
Fruited bubbly wines will complement the sweet glaze and earthy spiciness of the coating.

Aromatic spices, seeds and nuts combine to make an exotic coating with as much texture as taste. Expect an exhilarating eating experience that alludes to Middle Eastern tradition.

Chicken Saltimbocca Spikes

Finely chopped fresh sage	2 tbsp.	30 mL
Pepper	1/8 tsp.	0.5 mL
Chicken breast fillets, cut crosswise into 3 pieces each	1/2 lb.	225 g
Prosciutto ham slices, cut lengthwise into 1 inch (2.5 cm) wide strips	3 oz.	85 g
Fresh sage leaves	8	8
Butter, melted	2 tbsp.	30 mL
Extra-virgin olive oil	1 tbsp.	15 mL
Marsala wine	2 tbsp.	30 mL
Bamboo cocktail picks or skewers, approximately	18	18
Lemon juice	2 tbsp.	30 mL

Sprinkle sage and pepper on chicken. Roll 1 prosciutto strip around each chicken piece. Place, seam-side down, in a baking dish.

Scatter sage leaves over rolls. Drizzle with butter and olive oil. Bake in a 450°F (230°C) oven for 4 minutes. Drizzle with marsala. Bake for about 4 minutes until internal temperature reaches 175°F (80°C).

Skewer rolls. Drizzle with lemon juice and pan juices. Makes about 18 spikes.

1 spike: 45 Calories; 2.7 g Total Fat (0.9 g Mono, 0.2 g Poly, 1.1 g Sat); 14 mg Cholesterol; 1 g Carbohydrate; trace Fibre; 4 g Protein; 143 mg Sodium

---

GARNISH
cooked sage leaves
lemon slices

PRESENTATION INSPIRATION
To make an inventive stand for your skewers, simply cut a lemon in half lengthwise, place it cut-side down on a plate, and securely lodge the skewers in the lemon.

ABOUT SALTIMBOCCA
Although this version uses chicken, saltimbocca is a traditional Italian dish with veal, sage, prosciutto and marsala wine.

Full Italian **flavours** of fresh sage and prosciutto **heighten** the **senses**. Marsala's fortified **sweetness** is the perfect **complement**. A finishing touch of lemon **enlivens**, and the creation is **complete**.

Thai Chicken
On Lemon Grass Skewers

Lean ground chicken	3/4 lb.	340 g
Fine dry bread crumbs	2/3 cup	150 mL
Brown sugar, packed	1 tbsp.	15 mL
Chopped fresh cilantro	1 tbsp.	15 mL
Minced lemon grass, bulb only (root and stalk removed)	1 tbsp.	15 mL
Thai green curry paste	1 tbsp.	15 mL
Garlic clove, minced	1	1
Stalks of lemon grass, outer layers removed	6	6
Sesame oil	2 tbsp.	30 mL

Combine first 7 ingredients.

Press about 1/4 cup (60 mL) chicken mixture around each lemon grass stalk, about 1 inch (2.5 cm) from thick end. Brush with sesame oil. Cook on a greased grill on medium-high for about 15 minutes, turning often, until chicken is no longer pink (see Tip, below). Makes 6 skewers.

1 skewer: 214 Calories; 13.2 g Total Fat (2.1 g Mono, 2.0 g Poly, 0.9 g Sat); 0 mg Cholesterol; 12 g Carbohydrate; trace Fibre; 11 g Protein; 226 mg Sodium

---

GARNISH
sprigs of fresh cilantro

TIP
When grilling the skewers, make sure the lemongrass stalk ends are away from the heat. If the ends are too close to the fire or burner, they will be scorched.

ABOUT LEMON GRASS
Lemon grass contains one of the same essential oils that is found in lemon peel. This oil gives the grass that distinctive lemony aroma and flavour.

Fragrant lemon flavour **permeates** curry-flavoured chicken from the inside out with the help of lemon grass skewers. The novel **presentation** is bound to be a topic of conversation.

Leek-Wrapped Ginger Scallops
With Soy Glaze

Soy sauce	1/2 cup	125 mL
Brown sugar, packed	2 tbsp.	30 mL
Large leek (white part only), trimmed to 5 inches (12.5 cm)	1	1
Pickled ginger slices, halved	6	6
Large sea scallops	12	12
Wooden cocktail picks	12	12
Water	1/2 cup	125 mL
Soy sauce	2 tbsp.	30 mL

Combine first amount of soy sauce and brown sugar in a saucepan. Simmer on medium-low for about 5 minutes until reduced to a syrupy consistency.

Remove 12 leaves from centre of leek. Blanch in boiling water for 1 minute to soften. Drain and plunge into ice water for 1 minute. Drain well and blot dry.

Roll 1 ginger piece and 1 scallop in each leaf. Secure with cocktail picks (see How To, below).

Combine water and second amount of soy sauce in a frying pan. Bring to a simmer on medium and add skewers. Cook, covered, for about 4 minutes until scallops are opaque. Transfer to a serving plate using a slotted spoon. Serve with brown sugar mixture. Makes 12 skewers.

1 skewer with 1 tsp. (5 mL) glaze: 30 Calories; 0.1 g Total Fat (trace Mono, trace Poly, trace Sat); 5 mg Cholesterol; 4 g Carbohydrate; trace Fibre; 3 g Protein; 590 mg Sodium

**HOW TO ASSEMBLE
SCALLOP ROLLS**

Whereas bacon-wrapped scallops may be too much of a **good** thing, **leek-wrapped** scallops provide the **perfect** light compromise. The **inclusion** of ginger and a salty-sweet **glaze** finish off this small plate **perfectly**.

Rosemary-Spiked Meatballs

Lean ground lamb	1/2 lb.	225 g
Grated Greek Myzithra cheese	1/4 cup	60 mL
Large egg, fork-beaten	1	1
Sun-dried tomato pesto	2 tsp.	10 mL
Grated lemon zest	1 tsp.	5 mL
Chopped fresh rosemary	1 tsp.	5 mL
Sprigs of fresh rosemary (6 inches, 15 cm, each), see Tip, below	4	4

Combine first 6 ingredients. Roll into 12 balls and place on a baking sheet. Bake in a 400°F (205°C) oven for about 12 minutes until internal temperature reaches 160°F (70°C). Let stand until cool enough to handle.

Thread 3 meatballs onto each rosemary sprig. Makes 4 skewers.

1 skewer: 199 Calories; 15.2 g Total Fat (6.0 g Mono, 1.2 g Poly, 6.7 g Sat); 91 mg Cholesterol; 2 g Carbohydrate; trace Fibre; 13 g Protein; 375 mg Sodium

GARNISH
lemon wedges

TIP
When preparing your rosemary skewers, remove all the leaves, except for those on the last two inches of each stem. Use the removed leaves in the recipe.

PRESENTATION INSPIRATION
Serve your lamb skewers on a bed of couscous or bulgur for a more rustic appearance.

IMBIBE!
Your best bet for these skewers is a bold red wine, such as a shiraz, rioja or cabernet.

Rosemary's **heady aroma** permeates the air when its sprigs stand in place of skewers for these **Greek-inspired** lamb meatballs. A tzatziki dip can provide the **perfect** accompaniment.

Mahogany Chicken Waves

Brown sugar, packed	2 tbsp.	30 mL
Chili powder	1 tbsp.	15 mL
Smoked sweet paprika	1 tbsp.	15 mL
Cocoa, sifted if lumpy	1 tsp.	5 mL
Garlic powder	1/4 tsp.	1 mL
Pepper	1/4 tsp.	1 mL
Boneless, skinless chicken breast halves (4 – 6 oz., 113 – 170 g, each), cut lengthwise into 4 strips each	2	2
Bamboo skewers (8 inches, 20 cm, each), soaked in water for 10 minutes	8	8
Olive oil	1 tbsp.	15 mL
Salt	1/2 tsp.	2 mL

Combine first 6 ingredients. Add chicken and stir. Chill, covered, for 1 hour.

Thread chicken onto skewers. Brush with olive oil and sprinkle with salt. Cook on a greased grill on medium for about 3 minutes per side until no longer pink inside. Makes 8 skewers.

1 skewer: 107 Calories; 3.0 g Total Fat (1.6 g Mono, 0.5 g Poly, 0.6 g Sat); 39 mg Cholesterol; 4 g Carbohydrate; trace Fibre; 15 g Protein; 195 mg Sodium

---

GARNISH
lime wedges

ABOUT SMOKED PAPRIKA
Smoked Spanish paprika (or *pimentón*) is a much different product than regular paprika. It is made by slowly smoking pimientos over oak. It comes in three varieties: mild and sweet (*dulce*); medium bittersweet (*agridulce*); and hot (*picante*). It is most notably used in chorizo sausage and paella.

A cocoa and **smoked sweet** paprika rub lends a **becoming** mahogany hue to **thin strips** of chicken threaded in waves. The presentation is **memorable**, and so is the **bittersweet** taste.

Beef
With Pineapple Mustard

Pineapple juice	2 cups	500 mL
Brown sugar, packed	1/4 cup	60 mL
Dijon mustard	2 tbsp.	30 mL
Salt	1/8 tsp.	0.5 mL
Pepper	1/4 tsp.	1 mL
Cooking oil	1 tsp.	5 mL
Seasoned salt	1/2 tsp.	2 mL
Pepper	1/4 tsp.	1 mL
Beef tenderloin, trimmed and cut into 1 inch (2.5 cm) cubes	1/2 lb.	225 g
Pineapple pieces (1 inch, 2.5 cm, each)	12	12
Bamboo skewers (8 inches, 20 cm, each), soaked in water for 10 minutes	4	4

Combine pineapple juice and sugar in a saucepan. Boil gently on medium for about 30 minutes until reduced to about 1/2 cup (125 mL).

Stir in next 3 ingredients. Reserve half of mustard mixture.

Combine next 3 ingredients. Add beef and toss.

Thread beef and pineapple onto skewers. Cook on a greased grill on medium-high for about 6 minutes, turning once and brushing with remaining mustard mixture, until they reach desired doneness. Serve with reserved mustard mixture. Makes 4 skewers.

1 skewer with 1 tbsp. (15 mL) mustard: 220 Calories; 4.4 g Total Fat (1.9 g Mono, 0.5 g Poly, 1.3 g Sat); 21 mg Cholesterol; 37 g Carbohydrate; 1 g Fibre; 9 g Protein; 373 mg Sodium

---

ALTERNATIVE METHOD
If you'd rather forgo the grill, these skewers can be easily broiled. Your food will cook in about the same amount of time as on the barbecue—just don't forget to turn and baste as directed. Set your oven rack so that the food is about 3 to 4 inches (7.5 to 10 cm) away from the top element. In most ovens, this is the top position.

Although the **simple beef** skewers will be done to **perfection,** it is the accompanying condiment that will take **centre stage.** We suggest you try it with **chicken** and **pork** as well.

Chili-Crusted Medallions

Large egg, fork-beaten	1	1
Lean ground pork	1/2 lb.	225 g
Uncooked shrimp (peeled and deveined), coarsely chopped	6 oz.	170 g
Fine dry bread crumbs	1/4 cup	60 mL
Cornstarch	1 tbsp.	15 mL
Seasoned salt	1/2 tsp.	2 mL
Chili paste (sambal oelek)	1/4 cup	60 mL
Wooden cocktail skewers	12	12
Plain yogurt	1/2 cup	125 mL

Combine first 6 ingredients. Shape into twelve 2 inch (5 cm) diameter patties and place on a greased baking sheet. Brush with chili paste. Broil for about 3 minutes until browned. Turn and brush with chili paste. Broil for about 4 minutes until browned and internal temperature reaches 160°F (70°C). Let stand for 5 minutes.

Insert cocktail skewers and place on a serving plate. Serve with yogurt. Makes 12 skewers.

1 skewer with 1 tbsp. (15 mL) yogurt: 93 Calories; 5.4 g Total Fat (2.2 g Mono, 0.6 g Poly, 2.1 g Sat); 52 mg Cholesterol; 3 g Carbohydrate; trace Fibre; 7 g Protein; 226 mg Sodium

EXPERIMENT!
Instead of sambal oelek, you can use any type of hot sauce you like. Grocery stores have a mind-boggling number of varieties that differ based on their heat, the type of pepper used and other ingredients, such as roasted peppers and garlic. Changing your sauce will subtly change the taste.

Made to be **dipped**, these miniature shrimp and pork patties have a **fiery presence** that begs for the relief of **cool yogurt**. Not for the **faint-hearted**, these small eats should be reserved for your most **flame-proofed** guests.

Sesame Chili Vegetable Skewers

Red pepper pieces, 1 inch (2.5 cm) each	32	32
Peeled jicama pieces, 1 inch (2.5 cm) wide, 1/4 inch (6 mm) thick	8	8
Small whole white mushrooms	8	8
Onion pieces, 1 inch (2.5 cm) each	8	8
Zucchini slices (with peel), 1/2 inch (12 mm) thick	8	8
Bamboo skewers (6 inches, 15 cm, each), soaked in water for 10 minutes	8	8
Sesame oil	1/3 cup	75 mL
Thai hot chili pepper (see Tip, page 110), minced	1	1
Finely grated gingerroot	2 tsp.	10 mL
Granulated sugar	2 tsp.	10 mL
Salt	1/2 tsp.	2 mL

Thread first 5 ingredients onto skewers.

Combine remaining 5 ingredients. Cook skewers on a greased grill on medium for 10 to 15 minutes, brushing occasionally with sesame oil mixture, until vegetables are tender-crisp. Brush with sesame oil mixture and transfer to a serving plate. Makes 8 skewers.

1 skewer: 104 Calories; 9.1 g Total Fat (3.5 g Mono, 3.8 g Poly, 1.3 g Sat); 0 mg Cholesterol; 6 g Carbohydrate; 1 g Fibre; 1 g Protein; 149 mg Sodium

---

PRESENTATION INSPIRATION

The way you cut your vegetables can greatly affect presentation. Crinkle cutters can be used, and even just cutting at a different angle can show you care enough to think about how your food is displayed. But when working with skewers, make sure each vegetable piece is cut roughly the same size to ensure even cooking.

These chili and ginger-basted vegetable skewers provide a colourful complement to any array of small plates. The crisp pieces of jicama are especially well-suited to the Asian-inspired baste.

Tuna Skewers

Soy sauce	2 tbsp.	30 mL
Sesame oil	2 tbsp.	30 mL
Pepper	1/2 tsp.	2 mL
Tuna steak, cut into 1 inch (2.5 cm) cubes	1 lb.	454 g
Finely chopped pistachios toasted (see How To, page 208)	1/2 cup	125 mL
Bamboo skewers (8 inches, 20 cm, each), soaked in water for 10 minutes	6	6

Combine first 3 ingredients in a large resealable freezer bag. Add tuna and marinate for 30 minutes in refrigerator. Drain, discarding marinade.

Press tuna into pistachios until coated. Thread onto skewers. Cook on a greased grill on medium-high for about 1 minute per side until browned. Makes 6 skewers.

1 skewer: 181 Calories; 10.1 g Total Fat (4.5 g Mono, 3.6 g Poly, 1.5 g Sat); 36 mg Cholesterol; 3 g Carbohydrate; 1 g Fibre; 19 g Protein; 292 mg Sodium

ABOUT TUNA
If you are someone who does not enjoy rare meat, fresh tuna is not the dish for you. Tuna is always served rare, or at the most, medium-rare. Tuna will become quite tasteless if it is overcooked.

Perhaps the ultimate in **decadent barbecue** fare, these pistachio-crusted **tuna** skewers are sure to be met with **delighted** exclamations of **approval**.

Bourbon Chicken Skewers

Orange juice	1 cup	250 mL
Brown sugar, packed	1/4 cup	60 mL
Bourbon whiskey	1/4 cup	60 mL
Soy sauce	2 tbsp.	30 mL
Cayenne pepper	1/4 tsp.	1 mL
Boneless, skinless chicken thighs (about 3 oz., 85 g, each), cut in half lengthwise	4	4
Bamboo skewers (8 inches, 20 cm, each), soaked in water for 10 minutes	8	8

Combine first 5 ingredients in a medium resealable freezer bag. Add chicken and marinate in refrigerator for at least 6 hours or overnight. Drain marinade into a saucepan. Boil gently on medium for about 20 minutes until thickened and syrupy.

Thread chicken onto skewers. Cook on a greased grill on medium for about 8 minutes, turning once and brushing with marinade, until no longer pink inside. Makes 8 skewers.

1 skewer: 119 Calories; 3.3 g Total Fat (1.2 g Mono, 0.8 g Poly, 0.9 g Sat); 28 mg Cholesterol; 10 g Carbohydrate; trace Fibre; 8 g Protein; 226 mg Sodium

---

GARNISH
sprigs of fresh mint

ABOUT BOURBON
Although bourbon shares its name with royalty in France, it is made in the United States. The rules governing the production of bourbon are quite strict: It must have a minimum of 51 percent corn grain and it must be aged for a minimum of two years in charred, white oak barrels. There are no hard and fast rules about which type of glass is best suited to bourbon, but some connoisseurs feel a brandy snifter is the best choice for full sensory impact.

Drenched in a cayenne, citrus and bourbon marinade, these skewers are bound to evoke images of sultry southern nights.

Pork Souvlaki
With Red Pepper Yogurt

Red wine	1/4 cup	60 mL
Olive oil	3 tbsp.	50 mL
Greek seasoning	2 tbsp.	30 mL
Garlic cloves, minced	3	3
Lemon juice	1 tbsp.	15 mL
Pork tenderloin, cut into 1 inch (2.5 cm) pieces	3/4 lb.	340 g
Bamboo skewers (4 inches, 10 cm, each), soaked in water for 10 minutes	6	6
Greek pita breads (7 inch, 18 cm, diameter)	3	3
Plain yogurt	1/2 cup	125 mL
Chopped roasted red pepper	2 tbsp.	30 mL
Greek seasoning	1 tbsp.	15 mL

Combine first 5 ingredients in a medium resealable freezer bag. Add pork and marinate in refrigerator for 2 hours. Drain, discarding marinade (see Tip, below).

Thread pork onto skewers. Cook on a greased grill on medium for about 5 minutes per side until meat reaches desired doneness.

Grill pita breads for 1 to 2 minutes per side until heated through. Cut into 6 pieces each. Arrange on a serving plate with pork skewers.

Combine remaining 3 ingredients. Serve with pork skewers and pita. Serves 6.

1 serving: 190 Calories; 6.1 g Total Fat (3.6 g Mono, 0.7 g Poly, 1.3 g Sat); 36 mg Cholesterol; 17 g Carbohydrate; 1 g Fibre; 15 g Protein; 350 mg Sodium

TIP
If you want to baste your skewers with any leftover marinade, it is important it be boiled first. Doing this will prevent any contamination from the raw meat. Never save and reuse uncooked marinade.

PRESENTATION INSPIRATION
For a clever serving vessel for your red pepper yogurt, remove the side (or top) third of a red pepper. Remove all ribs and seeds, and wash. Then fill the red pepper with the yogurt and include a small spoon.

Cooked **traditionally** on skewers, this **simple** Greek fare is elevated to **gourmet** proportions with an accompanying yogurt dip flavoured with **savoury**, roasted red peppers and Mediterranean **seasonings**.

Candied Chicken Sticks

Ingredient	Imperial	Metric
Maple syrup	1/2 cup	125 mL
Chili garlic sauce	2 tbsp.	30 mL
Indonesian sweet soy sauce	2 tbsp.	30 mL
Boneless, skinless chicken breast halves, cut lengthwise into 1/4 inch (6 mm) thick slices	1/2 lb.	225 g
Bamboo skewers (8 inches, 20 cm, each), soaked in water for 10 minutes	8	8
Finely shredded suey choy (Chinese cabbage), lightly packed	2 cups	500 mL
Green onions, cut into 3 inch (7.5 cm) lengths	2	2
Rice vinegar	1 tbsp.	15 mL

Combine first 3 ingredients. Reserve 1/4 cup (60 mL) syrup mixture. Combine chicken and remaining syrup mixture in a medium resealable freezer bag. Marinate in refrigerator for at least 6 hours or overnight. Drain, discarding marinade.

Thread chicken onto skewers. Cook on a well-greased grill on medium for 1 to 2 minutes per side until chicken is glazed and no longer pink inside. Brush with 2 tbsp. (30 mL) reserved syrup mixture.

Toss cabbage and green onion together on a serving platter.

Stir vinegar into remaining syrup mixture and drizzle over cabbage mixture. Top with skewers. Serves 4.

1 serving: 125 Calories; 4.4 g Total Fat (1.6 g Mono, 1.0 g Poly, 1.2 g Sat); 37 mg Cholesterol; 10 g Carbohydrate; 1 g Fibre; 11 g Protein; 243 mg Sodium

---

GARNISH
toasted sesame seeds

ABOUT SOAKING SKEWERS
It is important to properly soak the skewers before grilling so they don't burn or, worse yet, light on fire. The soaking will also prevent them from leaving any dry splinters in the meat.

Maple syrup and Indonesian sweet soy sauce give these chicken skewers a delicious, yet intangible, sweetness. Your guests will find the flavours familiar, yet somehow exotic and elusive.

Enticing. Do you ever really believe people who say they aren't partial to sweets? You know that deep inside they secretly yearn for something to lift their spirits and stir their senses. Why not put that resolve to the test? You might ask, "Just a small bite?" You know, and they'll soon learn, that one small bite of these tantalizing delicacies—silky custards, molten kisses, stunning trifles— is enough to capture their affections and have them in blissful surrender forever.

Small & Sweet

Petite yet powerful dessert temptations

Halvah Ice Cream Sundaes
With Orange Honey Figs

Vanilla halvah, cut into 1/2 inch (12 mm) pieces	1/2 cup	125 mL
Vanilla ice cream, softened	1 cup	250 mL
Dried figs, chopped	4	4
Orange juice	1/2 cup	125 mL
Liquid honey	3 tbsp.	50 mL
Vanilla sesame snaps, crushed	1/3 cup	75 ml

Freeze halvah for about 10 minutes until very firm. Stir into ice cream. Freeze for about 1 1/2 hours until firm.

Combine next 3 ingredients in a saucepan. Simmer on medium-low until reduced to a syrupy consistency. Let stand until cool.

Scoop ice cream mixture onto 4 small plates. Sprinkle about 2 tsp. (10 mL) sesame snaps on 1 side of ice cream and spoon fig mixture on opposite side. Sprinkle remaining sesame snaps over top. Makes 4 sundaes.

1 sundae: 392 Calories; 16.0 g Total Fat (trace Mono, 0.1 g Poly, 6.4 g Sat); 60 mg Cholesterol; 57 g Carbohydrate; 3 g Fibre; 7 g Protein; 84 mg Sodium

---

GARNISH
grated orange zest

ABOUT HALVAH
This Middle Eastern confection is typically made from sesame seeds and honey and occasionally includes chopped dried fruit or pistachio nuts. It's readily available in wrapped bars or long slabs from which individual slices can be cut. Variations of halvah exist in different regions including Asia and continental Europe. You may also find halvah made from a variety of other ingredients such as sunflower seeds, various nuts, beans, lentils and vegetables, including carrots, pumpkins, yams and squash.

Transport your guests to the Middle East with this **sweet** combination of halvah, ice cream and syrupy figs. **Mysterious** and **adventurous**, it's the **perfect** blend of **texture** contrasts.

Crisp Cinnamon Banana Boats

Small bananas, peeled and trimmed to 4 inches (10 cm) each	4	4
Flour tortillas (6 inch, 15 cm, diameter)	4	4
Butter, melted	1/4 cup	60 mL
Granulated sugar	1/4 cup	60 mL
Ground cinnamon	2 tsp.	10 mL
Caramel Irish cream liqueur	3 tbsp.	50mL
Chocolate hazelnut spread	3 tbsp.	50mL
Caramel (or butterscotch) ice cream topping	2/3 cup	150 mL

Place 1 banana on each tortilla. Fold in sides and roll up tightly from bottom to enclose. Secure with wooden picks (see How To, below).

Brush with melted butter and roll in a mixture of sugar and cinnamon. Place on a baking sheet. Bake in a 450°F (230°C) oven for about 8 minutes until golden. Cut in half diagonally.

Whisk liqueur and chocolate spread together until smooth. Drizzle onto a serving plate. Drizzle with ice cream topping. Arrange rolls over top. Serves 8.

1 serving: 303 Calories; 9.5 g Total Fat (2.4 g Mono, 0.6 g Poly, 4.5 g Sat); 15 mg Cholesterol; 52 g Carbohydrate; 2 g Fibre; 3 g Protein; 294 mg Sodium

HOW TO ROLL TORTILLAS

There's something **infatuating** about the combination of bananas and caramel. Maybe it's the **silky smoothness**, maybe the **sweetness**. Whatever the appeal, it's nothing less than **heavenly**.

Cappuccino Meringue Stack

Icing (confectioner's) sugar	2 tbsp.	30 mL
Instant coffee granules, crushed to a fine powder	2 tsp.	10 mL
Cornstarch	1 1/2 tsp.	7 mL
Skim milk powder	1 1/2 tsp.	7 mL
Ground cinnamon, just a pinch		
Egg whites (large), room temperature	2	2
Brown sugar, packed	2 tbsp.	30 mL
Vanilla extract	1/2 tsp.	2 mL
Semi-sweet chocolate baking square (1 oz., 28 g), chopped	1	1

Combine first 5 ingredients.

Beat egg whites until soft peaks form. Gradually add brown sugar, beating until stiff peaks form. Fold in vanilla and coffee mixture. Spoon into a large freezer bag with a piece snipped off 1 corner. Pipe onto a parchment paper-lined baking sheet in a spiral pattern, leaving a 1/2 inch (12 mm) space between each round (see How To, below). Bake in a 250°F (120°C) oven for 1 1/2 hours. Let stand on baking sheet set on a wire rack until cool. Break into pieces and stack on a large plate.

Microwave chocolate on medium (50%) for about 1 minute, stirring every 15 seconds, until almost melted. Stir until smooth. Drizzle over meringue stack. Serves 6.

1 serving: 62 Calories; 1.3 g Total Fat (0 g Mono, 0 g Poly, 0.8 g Sat); trace Cholesterol; 11 g Carbohydrate; trace Fibre; 2 g Protein; 23 mg Sodium

HOW TO PIPE AND BREAK MERINGUE

Melt-in-your-mouth meringue is given a **twist** with the addition of coffee, chocolate and just a **hint** of **cinnamon**. It's light on the palate, but certainly gets **top grades** for its refined **flavour**.

Raspberry Crème Brûlée

Seedless raspberry jam	1/3 cup	75 mL
Raspberry liqueur	1 tbsp.	15 mL
Whipping cream	1 1/2 cups	375 mL
White chocolate baking squares (1 oz., 28 g, each), chopped	4	4
Egg yolks (large)	4	4
Granulated sugar	2 tbsp.	30 mL
Raspberry liqueur	1 tbsp.	15 mL
Granulated sugar	1/4 cup	60 mL

Place 4 greased 6 oz. (175 mL) ramekins in a 9 x 9 inch (22 x 22 cm) baking pan. Whisk jam and liqueur together until smooth. Spoon into ramekins and chill for about 30 minutes until firm.

Heat cream in a saucepan on medium until bubbles form around edge of pan. Remove from heat. Add chocolate and stir until melted.

Whisk next 3 ingredients together. Gradually whisk into cream mixture. Carefully pour into ramekins (see How To, below). Pour boiling water into pan until water comes halfway up sides of ramekins. Bake in a 300°F (150°C) oven for about 50 minutes until centres only wobble slightly. Transfer ramekins to a wire rack to cool completely. Chill, covered, for at least 6 hours or overnight.

Sprinkle 1 tbsp. (15 mL) sugar over each. Broil for about 5 minutes until sugar is browned and bubbling. Let stand for 5 minutes before serving. Makes 4 crème brûlées.

1 crème brûlée: 665 Calories; 46.3 g Total Fat (11.3 g Mono, 1.8 g Poly, 27.0 g Sat); 310 mg Cholesterol; 56 g Carbohydrate; 0 g Fibre; 7 g Protein; 69 mg Sodium

HOW TO POUR CUSTARD INTO RAMEKINS
In order to avoid disturbing the jam layer, carefully pour the custard over the back of a spoon.

GARNISH
fresh raspberries

There's **treasure** hidden beneath a **crisp**, sugary crust.
Dig down to find the velvety splendour of raspberry,
chocolate and whipping cream. **Simple** preparation,
yet this dessert is nothing but **decadent**.

Caramel Rum S'Mores

Large marshmallows	6	6
Caramels	6	6
Whipping cream	1/4 cup	60 mL
Spiced rum	2 tbsp.	30 mL
Vanilla extract	1/2 tsp.	2 mL
Large marshmallows	8	8
Two-bite brownies	8	8
Cocktail picks or bamboo skewers	8	8

Microwave first 5 ingredients in a deep bowl (see Tip, below) on medium (50%) for about 5 minutes, stirring every 60 seconds, until almost melted. Stir until smooth. Cover to keep warm.

On a baking sheet, place 1 marshmallow over each brownie. Broil for about 1 minute until marshmallows are golden.

Push skewers through top of marshmallows and into brownies. Serve with caramel sauce. Makes 8 s'mores.

1 s'more with 1 tbsp. (15 mL) sauce: 184 Calories; 8.0 g Total Fat (0.9 g Mono, 0.4 g Poly, 3.0 g Sat); 19 mg Cholesterol; 26 g Carbohydrate; 1 g Fibre; 2 g Protein; 83 mg Sodium

---

TIP
Because marshmallows expand when microwaved, be sure to use a large, deep bowl when heating the marshmallows for the caramel sauce. If you prefer, use a double boiler instead and make the sauce on the stovetop.

PRESENTATION INSPIRATION
If you're invited to a campfire or hosting one yourself, why not add a touch of gourmet to the event? Gather some sticks for roasting marshmallows and surprise everyone with your idea. Have the caramel sauce made in advance or purchase some ready-made caramel sauce to use as a dip. Let everyone roast their own marshmallows and provide brownies and skewers so people can create their own special s'mores.

Brownies topped with **ooey, gooey** marshmallows, broiled and served with a **rum caramel sauce** for dipping. Sure to bring back memories of roasting marshmallows over a campfire.

Lavalicious Chocolate Kisses

Bittersweet chocolate baking square (1 oz., 28 g), chopped	1	1
Semi-sweet chocolate baking square (1 oz., 28 g), chopped	1	1
Butter	1/4 cup	60 mL
Large eggs	2	2
Icing (confectioner's) sugar	2/3 cup	150 mL
Vanilla extract	1 tsp.	5 mL
All-purpose flour	1/4 cup	60 mL

Heat first 3 ingredients in a saucepan on lowest heat, stirring often, until chocolate is almost melted. Remove from heat. Stir until smooth. Let stand for 10 minutes.

Whisk next 3 ingredients together. Stir in chocolate mixture until combined.

Stir in flour until just moistened. Spoon into a small freezer bag with a small piece snipped off 1 corner. Fill 12 greased 1 oz. (30 mL) ramekins 3/4 full. Bake in a 425°F (220°C) oven for about 6 minutes until edges are set but centres still look wet and wobble slightly.
Makes 12 kisses.

1 kiss: 104 Calories; 6.3 g Total Fat (1.3 g Mono, 0.3 g Poly, 3.6 g Sat); 41 mg Cholesterol; 11 g Carbohydrate; trace Fibre; 2 g Protein; 37 mg Sodium

GARNISH
sifted cocoa

ABOUT CHOCOLATE
Officially, there are three kinds of chocolate: dark, milk and white. Dark chocolate contains cocoa liquor, cocoa butter and sugar. The higher the cocoa content, the more bitter the chocolate. Milk chocolate contains the same ingredients as dark chocolate, with the addition of milk powder for a lighter colour with a creamier texture and taste. White chocolate contains milk, sugar and cocoa butter, but no cocoa liquor. That explains the pale, ivory colour of this sweet confection which, by many people's standards, does not fit the definition of chocolate at all.

Decadent little chocolate bites
with **molten** centres—
this is one kiss you **won't soon forget.**

Pomegranate Jellies

Envelope of unflavoured gelatin (about 1 tbsp., 15 mL)	1/4 oz.	7 g
Pomegranate juice	1 cup	250 mL
Water	1/4 cup	60 mL
Icewine	1/4 cup	60 mL
Granulated sugar	2 tbsp.	30 mL

Sprinkle gelatin over juice and water in a saucepan. Let stand for 1 minute.

Add icewine and sugar. Heat and stir until sugar is dissolved. Pour into 6 glasses or small dessert cups. Chill for about 3 hours until set. Serves 6.

1 serving: 60 Calories; 0 g Total Fat (0 g Mono, 0 g Poly, 0 g Sat); 0 mg Cholesterol; 13 g Carbohydrate; 0 g Fibre; trace Protein; 10 mg Sodium

---

GARNISH
fresh mint leaves
fresh raspberries
fresh strawberries

ABOUT ICEWINE
Icewine is made by picking overripe grapes that have frozen on the vine on a cold night. The grapes are then pressed before they thaw. Because the water in the grapes is still frozen, the juice is much more concentrated, resulting in an extremely sweet dessert wine. Because the process of making icewine is labour-intensive, the price tends to be quite high.

Definitely not a kid's dessert—this truly grown-up jelly is elevated to gourmet fare with the flavour of pomegranate and the addition of icewine.

Strawberry Mascarpone Trifles

Ladyfingers (about 4 inches, 10 cm, each)	6	6
Container of frozen strawberries in light syrup, thawed	15 oz.	425 g
Raspberry liqueur	2 tbsp.	30 mL
Mascarpone cheese	1 1/4 cups	300 mL
Icing (confectioner's) sugar	1/3 cup	75 mL

Break 1 ladyfinger into pieces and place in 1 cocktail glass or dessert dish. Repeat with remaining ladyfingers, using a separate glass for each.

In a blender or food processor, process strawberries and liqueur until smooth. Pour over ladyfingers, reserving a small amount for topping.

Combine cheese and icing sugar. Spoon into a small freezer bag and snip a small piece off 1 corner. Pipe over strawberry mixture and drizzle with remaining strawberry mixture. Makes 6 trifles.

1 trifle: 515 Calories; 44.4 g Total Fat (0.5 g Mono, 0.2 g Poly, 23.7 g Sat); 157 mg Cholesterol; 24 g Carbohydrate; trace Fibre; 8 g Protein; 68 mg Sodium

---

GARNISH
fresh strawberries
sprigs of fresh mint

ABOUT MASCARPONE
This rich, decadent cheese is made from the milk of cows that have been fed grasses with fresh herbs and flowers—a diet that creates a fresh and unique taste. The cow's milk is allowed to stand and, after rising naturally to the milk's surface, the cream is skimmed off, poured into metal containers and heated in a double boiler. A few more ingredients are added to thicken the mixture, giving mascarpone its rich, dense texture.

Sweet as can be and deeply **satisfying**.
Mascarpone cheese, strawberries, raspberry liqueur
and light, sweet **ladyfingers** make
this small sweet pure **perfection**.

Ginger-Poached Pears

Small, firm peeled pears	4	4
Water	3 cups	750 mL
Icewine	1 cup	250 mL
Granulated sugar	1/2 cup	125 mL
Lemon juice	2 tbsp.	30 mL
Piece of gingerroot (1 inch, 2.5 cm, length), chopped	1	1

Core pears from the bottom, leaving stems intact. Cut a thin slice from bottoms so pears will stand upright.

Combine remaining 5 ingredients in a large saucepan. Bring to a boil, stirring to dissolve sugar. Reduce heat to medium-low. Lay pears on their sides in pan. Simmer, covered, for 20 to 25 minutes, turning occasionally, until pears are tender when pierced with a knife. Transfer pears to a serving dish, using a slotted spoon. Remove and discard ginger. Boil poaching liquid on medium-high for about 20 minutes until reduced and slightly thickened. Serve with pears (see How To, below). Serves 4.

1 serving: 216 Calories; 0.2 g Total Fat (trace Mono, trace Poly, trace Sat); 0 mg Cholesterol; 47 g Carbohydrate; 4 g Fibre; 1 g Protein; 2 mg Sodium

HOW TO SLICE PEARS FOR A FLOWER PETAL APPEARANCE
For an attractive presentation, you can cut your pears so that they have a flower shape. Make several cuts around the pear, starting about halfway up and cutting through to the bottom. Cut just to the centre of the pear, where the core has been removed. Once you have made cuts all around the pear, gently spread out to make a flower shape.

GARNISH
chopped crystallized ginger
lemon peel

Ultra-sweet icewine is the **perfect** ingredient
for **poaching** pears. Paired with ginger and lemon,
it's one hot ticket to a **higher level** of taste.

Orange Ice Cream Sandwiches

Granulated sugar	1/3 cup	75 mL
Butter	1/4 cup	60 mL
Orange juice	1/4 cup	60 mL
Lemon juice	1 tbsp.	15 mL
Large egg, fork-beaten	1	1
Egg yolk (large)	1	1
Grated orange zest	2 tsp.	10 mL
Whipping cream	1/2 cup	125 mL
Orange liqueur	1 tbsp.	15 mL
Chocolate wafers	18	18

Cocoa, sifted if lumpy, sprinkle

Combine first 7 ingredients in a saucepan. Cook and stir on medium until thickened enough to coat the back of a spoon. Do not boil. Let stand until cool. Place plastic wrap directly on surface to prevent skin from forming. Chill for about 2 hours until cold.

Beat cream and liqueur until soft peaks form. Fold into orange mixture.

Place 8 wafers on a waxed paper-lined baking sheet. Spoon half of orange mixture over wafers. Top with wafers. Spoon remaining orange mixture over second layer of wafers. Break remaining 2 wafers into quarters and place 1 piece over each sandwich. Freeze for 1 hour.

Just before serving, dust with cocoa powder. Makes 8 sandwiches.

1 sandwich: 215 Calories; 14.1 g Total Fat (4.2 g Mono, 1.2 g Poly, 7.8 g Sat); 81 mg Cholesterol; 20 g Carbohydrate; 1 g Fibre; 2 g Protein; 133 mg Sodium

---

GARNISH
orange peel

This is one **ice cream sandwich** you won't find peddled by the ice cream man—It's no kiddie **confection**. It's **rich** as can be with **whipping** cream, chocolate and a touch of orange **liqueur**.

Vanillacotta

With Liqueur

Unflavoured gelatin	4 tsp.	20 mL
Cold water	3 tbsp.	50 mL
Whipping cream	1/2 cup	125 mL
Packet of vanilla sugar	1/4 oz.	9 g
Vanilla-bean flavoured yogurt (not fat-free)	1 cup	250 mL
Vanilla (or hazelnut) liqueur	1/2 cup	125 mL

Sprinkle gelatin over cold water in a saucepan. Let stand for 1 minute. Add cream and vanilla sugar. Heat and stir until sugar is dissolved. Remove from heat.

Whisk in yogurt until combined. Pour into 6 small glasses. Chill, covered, for at least 6 hours or overnight.

Pour liqueur over vanillacottas. Serves 6.

1 serving: 178 Calories; 7.3 g Total Fat (2.0 g Mono, 0.3 g Poly, 4.6 g Sat); 28 mg Cholesterol; 18 g Carbohydrate; 0 g Fibre; 2 g Protein; 35 mg Sodium

---

GARNISH
toasted hazelnuts (filberts)

HOW TO MAKE YOUR OWN VANILLA SUGAR
Vanilla sugar can be used in cakes, jams, cocktails and pretty much anything else that requires a touch of vanilla essence. To make your own vanilla sugar, place a vanilla bean in a jar and cover it with granulated sugar. Use more beans for larger jars of sugar. Let it sit for about two weeks before removing the bean. Afterwards, you can save the beans in a separate jar for future use.

When you get something as **sinfully rich** as this, you'll want it to last forever. Vanilla **mingles** with the **slight tang** of yogurt to provide **perfect** balance.

Mysterious. The chef knows the secrets—the right ingredients to use, the way to artfully style a plate and, perhaps, a shortcut or two to gourmet gratification. But guests will be completely fooled by exquisite tastes and textures, beckoning aromas and the visual display that both delights and tempts. It's far too divine to be simple, right? Easy Prosciutto-Wrapped Bread Sticks With Cantaloupe Purée and Strawberry Salsa With Goat Cheese And Melba Toast are just two of the dishes that will hold a dining audience captive, without holding you captive in the kitchen.

Simply Sophisticated

Ordinary foods dressed to the nines

Lemon Thyme Sorbet

Thin lemon slices	4	4
Water	1/2 cup	125 mL
Granulated sugar	3 tbsp.	50 mL
Sprigs of fresh thyme	2	2
Lemon juice	2 tbsp.	30 mL
Grated lemon zest	1/2 tsp.	2 mL
Finely chopped fresh thyme	1/2 tsp.	2 mL

Press lemon slices into 4 shot glasses and freeze.

Combine next 3 ingredients in a saucepan. Boil gently on medium for about 8 minutes. Remove and discard thyme sprigs.

Stir in remaining 3 ingredients. Let stand until slightly cooled. Pour into prepared shot glasses. Freeze for about 2 hours until firm. Serves 4.

1 serving: 38 Calories; trace Total Fat (0 g Mono, 0 g Poly, 0 g Sat); 0 mg Cholesterol; 10 g Carbohydrate; trace Fibre; trace Protein; trace Sodium

GARNISH
sprigs of fresh thyme

ABOUT SORBET
Sorbet is the perfect palate cleanser because, unlike sherbet and ice cream, it does not contain any dairy. This leaves it light and refreshing. Although sweet varieties are also popular for dessert, savoury flavours are being used more and more often as palate cleansers.

PRESENTATION INSPIRATION
A palate cleanser is simply meant to refresh the palate—not satiate your guests. A tiny scoop the size of a melon ball will suffice nicely. But how you present it gives you an opportunity to let your imagination soar. It can be served on a small block of ice, in a large wonton spoon or set atop crushed ice in an egg cup—just remember to always include a spoon.

Citrus sorbet makes a great palate cleanser when there are lots of different **flavours** vying for your taste buds' **attention**. A sorbet shooter is just enough to **refresh** the palate between small plates.

Calabrese Bites

Calabrese salami slices, halved (about 2 oz., 57 g)	6	6
Medium fresh basil leaves	12	12
Cherry tomatoes, halved	6	6
Small bocconcini cheese balls	12	12
Pieces of sun-dried tomato in oil, about 1/2 inch (12 mm) each	12	12
Wooden cocktail picks	12	12
Balsamic vinegar	1 tbsp.	15 mL
Coarsely ground pepper, sprinkle		

Arrange salami on work surface, placing 1 basil leaf over each piece. Place next 3 ingredients in a row over top. Fold up ends of salami and insert a wooden pick from end to end to secure (see How To, below). Place on a baking sheet.

Drizzle with balsamic vinegar. Bake in a 400°F (205°C) oven for about 3 minutes until hot. Sprinkle with pepper and serve immediately. Makes 12 bites.

1 bite: 95 Calories; 7.8 g Total Fat (0.3 g Mono, 0.1 g Poly, 2.7 g Sat); 16 mg Cholesterol; 1 g Carbohydrate; trace Fibre; 6 g Protein; 74 mg Sodium

HOW TO ASSEMBLE BITES

ALTERNATIVE METHOD
Instead of baking these bites, simply microwave on high for 15 to 20 seconds until hot.

GARNISH
sprigs of fresh basil

Evocative of a sunny Italian countryside picnic, these **exceptional** salami and **bocconcini** bites combine many of the fresh flavours so characteristic of Tuscany.

Curried Cheese And Fruit Wheel

Block of cream cheese, softened	4 oz.	125 g
Chopped dried apricot	1/4 cup	60 mL
Raisins, chopped	1/4 cup	60 mL
Madras curry paste	1 1/2 tsp.	7 mL
Finely chopped green onion	1 tsp.	5 mL
Chopped mango chutney	2 tbsp.	30 mL
Sliced natural almonds, toasted (see How To, page 208)	1 tbsp.	15 mL

Combine first 5 ingredients. Press firmly into a plastic wrap-lined 1 cup (250 mL) ramekin or bowl with straight sides. Invert onto a serving plate.

Spread with mango chutney and sprinkle with almonds. Serve immediately. Makes about 1 cup (250 mL).

2 tbsp. (30 mL): 91 Calories; 5.9 g Total Fat (1.7 g Mono, 0.3 g Poly, 3.1 g Sat); 15 mg Cholesterol; 9 g Carbohydrate; 1 g Fibre; 2 g Protein; 113 mg Sodium

---

ABOUT CURRY PASTES
To say that all curry pastes are equal would be like saying all white wines taste the same. Perhaps the only true thing we can say about them as a group is that they are all pastes. Usually they contain ghee (clarified butter), vinegar and spices, but the spices used can vary drastically. The spices are chosen to suit certain styles of cuisine or types of meat—which makes substituting one for another a very tricky proposition if you are unfamiliar with their individual characteristics.

Dried fruit and **mango** chutney make this **almond-sprinkled** cheese wheel a **vibrant** and flavoursome accompaniment for crackers, Walnut Ginger Crisps (page 80) or Savoury Shortbread Trio (page 76).

Braised Hoisin Spareribs

Sweet-and-sour-cut pork ribs (breastbone removed)	1 1/2 lbs.	680 g
Hoisin sauce	1/4 cup	60 mL
Sweet chili sauce	1/4 cup	60 mL
Sesame oil	2 tbsp.	30 mL
Soy sauce	2 tbsp.	30 mL
Water	2 tbsp.	30 mL
Garlic cloves, minced	2	2
Chinese five-spice powder	1 tsp.	5 mL

Place ribs, bone-side down, in a baking pan.

Stir remaining 7 ingredients until smooth. Pour 2/3 cup (150 mL) of sauce mixture over ribs. Bake, covered, in a 350°F (175°C) oven for 30 minutes. Bake, uncovered, for about 45 minutes, basting with pan juices and remaining sauce mixture, until fully cooked and tender. Cover with foil and let stand for 10 minutes. Transfer to cutting board and cut ribs into 1-bone portions. Makes about 12 ribs.

1 rib: 203 Calories; 15.8 g Total Fat (6.7 g Mono, 2.2 g Poly, 5.4 g Sat); 44 mg Cholesterol; 5 g Carbohydrate; trace Fibre; 10 g Protein; 420 mg Sodium

GARNISH
sliced green onion

ABOUT SWEET-AND-SOUR-CUT RIBS
Sweet-and-sour-cut ribs are simply spareribs (also known as side ribs) cut into two-inch portions. If you cannot easily find this cut, your local butcher will be glad to prepare it for you.

PRESENTATION INSPIRATION
The presentation of your food can be greatly improved simply by varying your cutting. In this recipe, consider cutting the green onion garnish on a sharp angle. It's easy and adds a special touch.

Hoisin and five-spice powder lend an **aromatic** Asian influence to these **small morsels** with a lively **chili heat**. Serve with finger bowls so your guests can engage in a more refined eating **experience**.

Prosciutto-Wrapped Bread Sticks
With Cantaloupe Purée

Coarsely chopped ripe cantaloupe	1 cup	250 mL
Ground cinnamon, just a pinch		
Thin slices of prosciutto ham	8	8
(about 4 oz., 113 g)		
Bread sticks (6 – 8 inches, 15 – 20 cm, each)	8	8

In a blender or food processor, process cantaloupe and cinnamon until smooth. Pour into 8 small glasses.

Wrap 1 slice of prosciutto around 1 end of each breadstick. Place 1 bread stick across rim of each glass. Serve immediately. Serves 8.

1 serving: 78 Calories; 2.5 g Total Fat (0.4 g Mono, 0.4 g Poly, 0.7 g Sat); 11 mg Cholesterol; 9 g Carbohydrate; trace Fibre; 5 g Protein; 444 mg Sodium

---

ABOUT CANTALOUPE
Although a cantaloupe's colour and texture will change after being picked, all its flavour comes from being allowed to properly ripen on the vine—so it is important to choose a ripe one. It should have a slightly musky odour because an odourless melon will lack flavour. Push on the melon's base, opposite the stem. It should give a little without being too soft. Soft and lumpy melons are past their prime and will be quite watery.

EXPERIMENT!
Try using seasoned bread sticks to vary the flavour. If they are too long, simply cut them in half before serving.

This modernized version of **classic** proscuitto-wrapped melon perfectly **balances** the salty ham with the **invigorating** **sweetness** of the cantaloupe purée. The varied textures also add a **sensual** dimension to the flavour **experience**.

Strawberry Salsa
With Goat Cheese And Melba Toast

Finely chopped fresh strawberries	2 cups	500 mL
White balsamic vinegar	2 tbsp.	30 mL
Minced fresh basil	1 1/2 tbsp.	25 mL
Minced fresh chives	1 1/2 tsp.	7 mL
Granulated sugar	1 tsp.	5 mL
Coarsely ground pepper	1/2 tsp.	2 mL
Soft goat (chèvre) cheese	1/4 cup	60 mL
Round Melba toasts	24	24

Combine first 6 ingredients. Let stand for 30 minutes to blend flavours.

Serve cheese with Melba toast and strawberry mixture. Serves 8.

1 serving: 89 Calories; 1.6 g Total Fat (0.4 g Mono, 0.3 g Poly, 0.8 g Sat); 2 mg Cholesterol; 16 g Carbohydrate; 2 g Fibre; 3 g Protein; 143 mg Sodium

ABOUT WHITE BALSAMIC VINEGAR
Less sweet and more mild than regular balsamic vinegar, the white variety will not overpower other flavours. It is made from white wine vinegar and concentrated grape juice.

TIP
When making salsas or chutneys, it is wise to let the flavours sit and blend properly rather than serving them as soon as they are made. In fact, these dishes are often considered more balanced and flavourful the next day. Simply prepare, cover and leave overnight in the refrigerator.

Balsamic vinegar and pepper highlight an often-overlooked aspect of fresh strawberries—their ability to blend well with, rather than overshadow, other ingredients. Further enhanced by chèvre, this ensemble is both captivating and surprising.

Chipotle Corn Soup

Butter	1 tsp.	5 mL
Chopped onion	1/2 cup	125 mL
Chopped chipotle pepper in adobo sauce (see Tip, below)	1 1/2 tsp.	7 mL
Prepared vegetable broth	1 1/2 cups	375 mL
Frozen kernel corn	1 1/2 cups	375 mL
Half-and-half cream	1/4 cup	60 mL
Salt	1/8 tsp.	0.5 mL

Melt butter in a saucepan on medium. Add onion and chipotle pepper and cook until onion is soft.

Add broth and corn. Simmer for about 10 minutes until corn is softened. Using a hand blender, process until smooth (see Safety Tip, page 40). Strain through a sieve, pressing solids with the back of a spoon. Discard solids.

Stir in cream and salt. Chill for about 4 hours until cold. Serves 4.

1 serving: 83 Calories; 3.1 g Total Fat (0.8 g Mono, 0.3 g Poly, 1.6 g Sat); 8 mg Cholesterol; 13 g Carbohydrate; 2 g Fibre; 2 g Protein; 221 mg Sodium

---

GARNISH
sprigs of fresh parsley

TIP
Store any leftover chipotle peppers in an airtight container in the fridge.

Chilled and **velvety smooth** yet contrasted with an **intense, smoky** chipotle pepper heat, this southwestern-influenced soup refreshes and **invigorates** all at once.

Coconut Lime Chicken Salad Cocktails

Coconut milk	1/2 cup	125 mL
Brown sugar, packed	1 tbsp.	15 mL
Lime juice	1 tbsp.	15 mL
Dried crushed chilies	1/2 tsp.	2 mL
Seasoned salt	1/2 tsp.	2 mL
Thinly sliced cooked chicken	1 1/3 cups	325 mL
Julienned carrot (see How To, below)	1/2 cup	125 mL
Thinly sliced red pepper, about 2 inch (5 cm) long slices	1/2 cup	125 mL
Arugula leaves, lightly packed	2 cups	500 mL

Whisk first 5 ingredients together until sugar is dissolved. Add next 3 ingredients and toss. Chill, covered, for 1 to 2 hours.

Arrange arugula in 6 martini or cocktail glasses. Spoon chicken mixture over top. Serves 6.

1 serving: 124 Calories; 7.2 g Total Fat (1.0 g Mono, 0.6 g Poly, 4.9 g Sat); 28 mg Cholesterol; 6 g Carbohydrate; 1 g Fibre; 10 g Protein; 157 mg Sodium

HOW TO JULIENNE
To julienne, cut into thin matchstick-like strips.

GARNISH
lime peel

This **inspired** salad cocktail delivers the **flavours** of the **tropics** presented in a most **unconventional** manner. **Whimsical** in presentation but seriously **delectable** in taste.

Tapenade Toasts

Baguette bread slices, cut at a sharp angle, about 1/2 inch (12 mm) thick	4	4
Olive oil	1 tbsp.	15 mL
Soft goat (chèvre) cheese	1/4 cup	60 mL
Black olive tapenade	1/4 cup	60 mL
Chopped fresh basil	1 tbsp.	15 mL

Arrange bread slices on a baking sheet. Brush with olive oil. Bake in a 350°F (175°C) oven for about 10 minutes until golden. Turn over and brush with olive oil. Bake for about 5 minutes until golden.

Spread with goat cheese and tapenade. Sprinkle with basil. Cut in half diagonally. Makes 8 toasts.

1 toast: 60 Calories; 5.1 g Total Fat (3.1 g Mono, 0.6 g Poly, 1.1 g Sat); 2 mg Cholesterol; 3 g Carbohydrate; trace Fibre; 1 g Protein; 126 mg Sodium

---

ABOUT TAPENADE

The original tapenade hailing from Provence was a purée of capers, olives, anchovies and olive oil. The result was a salty, full-bodied spread for bread. Today, a tapenade can contain many different ingredients—you can even purchase varieties based on the specific type of olive used. It is becoming more and more common to find combinations that stray away from the olive entirely, such as artichoke and red pepper tapenades.

A diagonal cut of a baguette can present a **perfect canvas** for **simple,** expertly chosen **ingredients.** This rustic **arrangement** belies the **sophistication** of flavours.

Nut, Cheese And Fruit Bites

Mixed baby greens	1 cup	250 mL
Small fresh strawberries, stems removed	12	12
Soft goat (chèvre) cheese	1/3 cup	75 mL
Large unpeeled pear, cut into 1/4 inch (6 mm) slices	1	1
Lemon juice	1 tbsp.	15 mL
Blue cheese, crumbled	3/4 cup	175 mL
Pecans, walnuts and hazelnuts, toasted (see How To, below)	1 cup	250 mL

Arrange mixed greens on a serving tray.

Make 2 crosscuts from tip of each strawberry, almost, but not quite, through to base. Spread cuts open and fill with goat cheese. Arrange over greens.

Toss pear slices in lemon juice. Top slices with blue cheese. Arrange over greens.

Arrange nuts over fruit. Serves 6.

1 serving: 268 Calories; 22.7 g Total Fat (9.5 g Mono, 5.6 g Poly, 5.1 g Sat); 16 mg Cholesterol; 11 g Carbohydrate; 4 g Fibre; 8 g Protein; 224 mg Sodium

---

HOW TO TOAST NUTS
Although raw nuts are perfectly fine for noshing, toasting them brings out an aroma and depth of flavour not apparent in the raw product. To toast nuts, seeds or coconut, place them in an ungreased frying pan. Heat on medium for 3 to 5 minutes, stirring often, until golden. To bake, spread them evenly in an ungreased shallow pan. Bake in a 350°F (175°C) oven for 5 to 10 minutes, stirring or shaking often, until golden.

This **colourful** small plate is only one **example** of how you can **showcase** your own exquisite culinary style. Serve your favourite fruits, cheeses and nuts in unlimited **combinations**. Let each individual taste come together and speak in **unison**.

Hot And Smoky Stuffed Dates

Medjool fresh whole dates, pitted	6	6
Real bacon bits	1 1/2 tsp.	7 mL
Asian chili sauce	3/4 tsp.	4 mL
Pieces of jalapeño Monterey Jack cheese, 1/4 inch (6 mm) thick, 1 1/2 inches (3.8 cm) long (about 3/4 oz., 21 g)	6	6
Roasted, salted smoked almonds	12	12

Stuff each date with 1/4 tsp. (1 mL) bacon bits, 1/8 tsp. (0.5 mL) chili sauce, and 1 piece of cheese. Place on a baking sheet.

Top with 2 almonds each. Bake in a 375°F (190°C) oven for about 10 minutes until cheese is melted. Let stand until slightly cooled. Serve with additional Asian Chili sauce. Makes 6 stuffed dates.

1 stuffed date: 53 Calories; 2.4 g Total Fat (0.8 g Mono, 0.3 g Poly, 0.7 g Sat); 3 mg Cholesterol; 7 g Carbohydrate; 1 g Fibre; 2 g Protein; 51 mg Sodium

---

GARNISH
sprig of parsley

ABOUT MEDJOOL DATES
The Medjool date is considered to be the king of dates due to its soft flesh, exceptional sweetness and large size—which makes it perfect for stuffing. Before stuffing, cut a 1 inch (2.5 cm) lengthwise slit in each date, and carefully remove and discard the pit.

ABOUT ASIAN CHILI SAUCES
Asian chili sauces distinguish themselves from North American hot sauces because they do not use tomato as a base. Instead they tend to use oils such as soy or palm, which makes their consistency more oily than smooth. They also usually include types of sugar that will give them a characteristic sweet heat.

Never has a more **varied** grouping of **flavours** and **textures** come together in such a small package. **Experience** salty, smoky, spicy, sweet, soft, chewy and crunchy sensations in a virtual **tempest of taste**.

Salty-Sweet Croustades

Walnut halves, toasted (see How To, page 208)	12	12
Liquid honey	3 tbsp.	50 mL
Baby green leaves	12	12
Pieces of Reggiano Parmigiano cheese, about 1/4 inch (6 mm) thick, 2 inches (5 cm) long (about 1/2 oz., 43 g)	12	12
Siljan mini croustade shells (see Tip, below)	12	12
Balsamic vinegar	1 tbsp.	15 mL

Coat walnuts with honey.

Place 1 lettuce leaf, 1 piece of cheese and 1 walnut in each croustade shell.

Drizzle with balsamic vinegar. Makes 12 croustades.

1 croustade: 45 Calories; 2.0 g Total Fat (0.3 g Mono, 1.0 g Poly, 0.5 g Sat); 2 mg Cholesterol; 6 g Carbohydrate; trace Fibre; 1 g Protein; 41 mg Sodium

---

TIP
Siljan croustade shells are generally found in the deli, import or cracker sections of your local grocery store.

ABOUT HONEY
In North America today, there are over 300 types of honey. By varying the honey you use, you will subtly vary the flavour. Each variety is based on the type of flower the particular honeybee colony gets its nectar from. Farmer's markets offer an excellent opportunity for trying different types—from blueberry to sourwood to eucalyptus. Of course, your local farmer's market will sell the varieties most common to your area.

A trip to an **Italian** market is bound to **motivate** anyone who loves to cook. This recipe was **inspired** by the Italian custom of combining sharp **Parmigiano** with the honest sweetness of **honey**.

Glossary

arborio rice ~ an Italian variety of short-grain rice used for making risotto. Kernels of arborio rice are shorter and fatter than other types of short-grain rice and have a very high starch content. The starch helps to give risotto its traditionally creamy texture.

capers ~ these small flower buds are picked from bushes native to the Mediterranean and parts of Asia. They are then sun-dried and pickled in brine. Capers range in size from the very small nonpareil to stemmed caperberries, which are the size of cocktail olives. Capers should be rinsed before using to remove excess salt.

cardamom ~ native to India, this aromatic spice is a member of the ginger family. Cardamom comes in small cranberry-sized pods. Although you can purchase cardamom already ground, for a fuller flavour it is better to use whole pods. For best results, crush the pods lightly with the back of a knife before using.

chard ~ you'll likely find several types of chard, this beet relative, at your produce market. Swiss chard will have crinkly green leaves with celery-like stalks, while ruby chard has deep green leaves with bright red stalks. You may also find rhubarb chard, which has lighter-coloured stalks and leaves. The leaves can be prepared much like spinach, while the stalks can be prepared like asparagus.

croustade shells ~ these little edible cups can be used to hold a variety of different fillings. They are made from pastry and are either baked or fried until crisp.

coconut milk ~ often used in curries, coconut milk can be quite rich and is made by combining equal parts of coconut meat and water. This mixture is simmered until foamy, then the coconut meat is strained and discarded.

coriander ~ known for both its seeds and leaves, which surprisingly taste nothing alike. The seeds are the dried ripened fruit of the plant and the leaves, also known as cilantro, are dark green and lacy. The seeds are used in baking, curries and pickling, or for beverages like mulled wines.

cumin ~ like coriander seed, cumin is a dried fruit from a plant in the parsley family. Aromatic and nutty, this spice is commonly found in curries and chili powders.

endive ~ often confused with chicory, endive comes in three main types. Belgian endive (sometimes known as French endive or witloof) comes in small cigar-shaped heads with tightly-packed leaves. It is grown in darkness to prevent the leaves from turning green, which accounts for its creamy colour. Curly endive grows in loosely packed heads of lacy green leaves. Escarole has broad, slightly curved leaves that are pale green. Belgian and curly endive have a slightly bitter taste, while the flavour of escarole tends to be a bit milder.

fennel ~ with a mild licorice flavour, the celery-like stems of this plant have a sweeter and more delicate flavour than anise, another licorice-flavoured ingredient. The feathery green leaves can be eaten, but are generally used only as a garnish or for a last-minute flavour boost. Fennel seed is also used for cooking, both in savoury and sweet dishes.

garam masala ~ a mixture of as many as twelve different spices, garam masala often includes black pepper, cardamom, cinnamon, cloves, coriander, cumin, dried chilies, fennel, mace and nutmeg. This blend is said to add warmth to both the spirit and the palate, which is fitting, since the Indian word garam literally means "warm."

green peppercorns ~ a young, soft pepper berry, generally preserved in brine, but occasionally packed in water. Green peppercorns can also be purchased freeze-dried. Because these berries are underripe, they tend to have a milder flavour than other types of pepper.

hoisin sauce ~ occasionally referred to as Peking sauce, this sweet and spicy sauce is often found in Chinese cooking. Made from soybeans, garlic, chili peppers and spices, this sauce is generally quite thick and is often used as a table condiment or to add flavour to meat dishes or stir-fries.

marjoram ~ an ancient herb, related to mint. When this ingredient is called for, sweet marjoram is what you're looking for (wild marjoram refers to oregano). The flavour is mild, sweet and somewhat similar to oregano. Another variety, pot marjoram, has a stronger and slightly bitter flavour.

mirin ~ a sweet wine, golden in colour and generally with low alcohol content. This ingredient is often used in Japanese cooking to add sweetness and flavour. Mirin is also sometimes known as rice wine.

miso ~ also known as bean paste, miso is an important ingredient in Japanese cuisine. Miso is made from fermented soy beans. The consistency is usually similar to peanut butter and is available in a variety of flavours and colours. Generally, lighter colours of miso are good for more delicately flavoured dishes, while darker colours work well with bolder flavours.

Old Bay seasoning ~ a blend of more than twelve herbs and spices, this mixture was created by a German-American immigrant named Gustav Brunn in 1939. The flavour of Old Bay seasoning is often associated with seafood, particularly crab.

olive oil ~ a flavourful and fragrant oil, often found in Mediterranean cooking. The flavour and colour of olive oil can vary depending upon growing region, crop condition and the process used to press or filter the oil. Generally, the deeper the colour of the oil, the more intense the flavour. Olive oils tend to have lower smoke-points than other oils, so be careful when frying.

panini bread ~ this Italian bread is generally quite thin and is used for grilled sandwiches. Translated, panini is Italian for "small bread."

panko bread crumbs ~ generally used for coating fried foods in Japanese cooking. Because they tend to be coarser than the bread crumbs used in North American cuisine, they create a perfectly crunchy crust.

pappadum ~ similar in appearance to a tortilla, this thin, wafer-like bread is made using lentil flour. You'll likely find pappadums in a variety of flavours and sizes in your grocery store or Indian market. They can either be fried, baked or grilled over an open flame.

plantain ~ often known as a cooking banana, the plantain is a large, firm variety of banana which must be cooked before eating. The colour of a plantain's skin will tell you which stage of ripeness it's at. Green is underripe, yellow is ripe and black is overripe. Plantains are consumed at all stages of ripeness and are generally very starchy.

polenta ~ similar to porridge, this cornmeal mixture hails from northern Italy. Very versatile, polenta can be eaten as a side dish or as a breakfast item, hot with butter or cooled until firm, then cut and fried. Polenta can also be flavoured with cheeses such as Parmesan or Gorgonzola. In your supermarket, you'll also find a firm version of polenta that can be sliced and grilled or fried.

prosciutto ~ translated from Italian, prosciutto quite simply means "ham." This type of ham is generally seasoned, salt-cured and dried. The meat is then pressed, which gives it a firm, dense texture. There are several varieties of prosciutto available, all of which are fine to eat without cooking. In fact, cooking prosciutto too much will toughen it, so it is best added at the last minute so it's just heated through.

rice paper rounds ~ these translucent papers are generally made from a mixture of water and rice flour. They come in a variety of sizes and shapes. Rice paper rounds are first rehydrated in hot water, then stuffed with fillings and served as-is or deep-fried.

salsa verde ~ generally a mixture of tomatillos, green chilies and cilantro, salsa verde literally means "green salsa."

sesame oil ~ there are two basic types of sesame oil. The lighter is good for a variety of applications from salad dressings to frying and has a nutty flavour. The darker variety is much stronger-tasting and is often used in Asian cooking to add flavour.

shallots ~ related to onions, shallots are favoured for their milder flavour. Shallots are cooked like onions, but they more closely resemble garlic in appearance. Shallots grow bulbs with multiple cloves, each separated by a papery skin. Fresh green shallots can be purchased seasonally, but red shallots are more commonly available.

suey choy ~ also known as Chinese cabbage, suey choy is cylindrical and has light green-coloured leaves. It's similar in flavour to bok choy.

tarragon ~ this aromatic herb has a flavour similar to anise and is commonly used in a variety of French dishes, including the well-known béarnaise sauce. Take care when using tarragon in your cooking, as its assertive flavour can easily overpower other ingredients.

wasabi paste ~ also known as Japanese horseradish, this green-coloured condiment has a sharp and spicy flavour. Sushi and sashimi are commonly served with a mixture of wasabi paste and soy sauce. Wasabi is made from the root of a plant related to horseradish. Some Asian markets may carry fresh wasabi, but powdered is also available.

Menu Suggestions

Sometimes matching flavours can be a tricky feat. We've taken away some of the guesswork and provided a few menu options based on either four or six guests. Be as creative as you like and select your own groupings, or use one of the following as a guide.

For 4

Chipotle Corn Soup, page 202
Seared Scallops Verde, page 92
Seta Antojitos Especial, page 132
Margarita Chicken Lollipops, page 68
Lavalicious Chocolate Kisses, page 176

Coconut Chili Soup, page 50
Smoked Tuna And
Wasabi Cream In Endive Boats, page 90
Braised Hoisin Spareribs, page 196
Miso Mushroom Risotto With Scallops, page 52
Ginger-Poached Pears, page 182

Seared Beef Carpaccio
With Peppercorn Mushrooms, page 58
Pannini Sticks With Dipping Trio, page 38
Praline Pecans, Beets And Blue Cheese
On Baby Greens, page 96
Raspberry Crème Brûlèe, page 172

For 6

Dukkah Beef Skewers
With Wine Reduction, page 138
Spiced Jam With Heady
Garlic and Cambozola, page 14
Tostada Cups With Lemony
Lentils and Spinach, page 20
Herb Olive Feta Mélange
Over Grilled Asparagus, page 108
Pomegranate Jellies, page 178

Butter Chicken With
Spinach And Pappadums, page 54
Walnut Ginger Crisps, page 80
Curried Cheese And Fruit Wheel, page 194
Curried Chicken Samosa Strudel, page 116
Vanillacotta With Liqueur, page 186

Prosciutto-Wrapped Bread Sticks
With Cantaloupe Purée, page 198
Tapenade Toasts, page 206
Calabrese Bites, page 192
Arugula Pesto Ravioli With
Browned Butter Pine Nuts, page 122
Sun-Dried Tomato And
Leek Mussels, page 42
Cappuccino Meringue Stack, page 170

Tip Index

Small Plates For Sharing - Index

Measurement Tables

Throughout this book measurements are given in Conventional and Metric measure. To compensate for differences between the two measurements due to rounding, a full metric measure is not always used. The cup used is the standard 8 fluid ounce. Temperature is given in degrees Fahrenheit and Celsius. Baking pan measurements are in inches and centimetres as well as quarts and litres. An exact metric conversion is given below as well as the working equivalent (Metric Standard Measure).

Oven Temperatures

Fahrenheit (°F)	Celsius (°C)	Fahrenheit (°F)	Celsius (°C)
175°	80°	350°	175°
200°	95°	375°	190°
225°	110°	400°	205°
250°	120°	425°	220°
275°	140°	450°	230°
300°	150°	475°	240°
325°	160°	500°	260°

Pans

Conventional - Inches	Metric - Centimetres
8 x 8 inch	20 x 20 cm
9 x 9 inch	22 x 22 cm
9 x 13 inch	22 x 33 cm
10 x 15 inch	25 x 38 cm
11 x 17 inch	28 x 43 cm
8 x 2 inch round	20 x 5 cm
9 x 2 inch round	22 x 5 cm
10 x 4 1/2 inch tube	25 x 11 cm
8 x 4 x 3 inch loaf	20 x 10 x 7.5 cm
9 x 5 x 3 inch loaf	22 x 12.5 x 7.5 cm

Spoons

Conventional Measure	Metric Exact Conversion Millilitre (mL)	Metric Standard Measure Millilitre (mL)
1/8 teaspoon (tsp.)	0.6 mL	0.5 mL
1/4 teaspoon (tsp.)	1.2 mL	1 mL
1/2 teaspoon (tsp.)	2.4 mL	2 mL
1 teaspoon (tsp.)	4.7 mL	5 mL
2 teaspoons (tsp.)	9.4 mL	10 mL
1 tablespoon (tbsp.)	14.2 mL	15 mL

Dry Measurements

Conventional Measure Ounces (oz.)	Metric Exact Conversion Grams (g)	Metric Standard Measure Grams (g)
1 oz.	28.3 g	28 g
2 oz.	56.7 g	57 g
3 oz.	85.0 g	85 g
4 oz.	113.4 g	125 g
5 oz.	141.7 g	140 g
6 oz.	170.1 g	170 g
7 oz.	198.4 g	200 g
8 oz.	226.8 g	250 g
16 oz.	453.6 g	500 g
32 oz.	907.2 g	1000 g (1 kg)

Cups

Conventional Measure	Metric Exact Conversion Millilitre (mL)	Metric Standard Measure Millilitre (mL)
1/4 cup (4 tbsp.)	56.8 mL	60 mL
1/3 cup (5 1/3 tbsp.)	75.6 mL	75 mL
1/2 cup (8 tbsp.)	113.7 mL	125 mL
2/3 cup (10 2/3 tbsp.)	151.2 mL	150 mL
3/4 cup (12 tbsp.)	170.5 mL	175 mL
1 cup (16 tbsp.)	227.3 mL	250 mL
4 1/2 cups	1022.9 mL	1000 mL (1 L)

Casseroles

Canada & Britain		United States	
Standard Size Casserole	Exact Metric Measure	Standard Size Casserole	Exact Metric Measure
1 qt. (5 cups)	1.13 L	1 qt. (4 cups)	900 mL
1 1/2 qts. (7 1/2 cups)	1.69 L	1 1/2 qts. (6 cups)	1.35 L
2 qts. (10 cups)	2.25 L	2 qts. (8 cups)	1.8 L
2 1/2 qts. (12 1/2 cups)	2.81 L	2 1/2 qts. (10 cups)	2.25 L
3 qts. (15 cups)	3.38 L	3 qts. (12 cups)	2.7 L
4 qts. (20 cups)	4.5 L	4 qts. (16 cups)	3.6 L
5 qts. (25 cups)	5.63 L	5 qts. (20 cups)	4.5 L

Our website is stuffed with all kinds of great information

www.companyscoming.com

Save up to 75% on cookbooks

Discover free recipes and cooking tips

Sign up for our free newsletter with exclusive offers

Preview new titles

Find older titles no longer in stores